MEMBERSHIP TO DISCIPLESHIP

GROWING MATURE DISCIPLES WHO MAKE DISCIPLES

PHIL MAYNARD

Membership to Discipleship: Growing Maturing Disciples Who Make Disciples of Jesus Christ

Copyright © 2015 by Dr. Phil Maynard

Paperback ISBN: 978-0-9899223-2-6

Printed in USA

This book is dedicated to

My daughter Amanda

Who also served as my proof-reader extraordinaire

My son Joshua

And

My Grandchildren:

Logan

Angel

Noah

Adam

Liam

For whom I pray that the Church

Will be the kind of place

Where they discover the abundant life

Of being a growing, maturing

Disciple of Jesus Christ

Table of Contents

Introduction

It is impossible to pick up any article about the future of the church or click on any church leadership blog on the web without reading dire observations about the decline in congregational participation in the past 20 years. The winds of change are blowing strongly, and the culture is shifting so rapidly that it's difficult to even keep up—writing illustrations for books like this one run a serious risk of passing from relevance before they even get published. Technology intimidates the members of committees established to rethink the trajectories of local congregations, and the erratic and intense swerves of pop culture can give these committee folk a severe case of whiplash.

It's not hard to feel sympathetic for the disoriented leaders of our local congregations. They are sincere. They love Jesus. They love their churches. They don't want to see their buildings shuttered and the members of their church family scattered to the winds. Many of them have been engaged in meaningful ministry on behalf of God's kingdom for decades. They still believe they have something to offer that is desperately needed by this world and its woes. If they can figure out what to do, they are willing to do it.

Discipleship matters. From the first days of regular people answering Jesus' call to "follow me," there has been a clear difference between those who listened eagerly to his voice and then moved on to the next thing and those who took the message to heart and devoted their lives to following the Master with passion so that the world might be changed. The church from time to time loses sight of what it means to serve as an incubator for those who would follow Jesus with "all their heart and soul and might." As with any highly structured bureaucracy, the church sometimes finds itself mired in a swamp of good intentions, fossilized structures, and misplaced priorities.

The way back to authentic discipleship, surprisingly, may not lie with the latest bells, whistles, or interactive video. The best path forward may be a return to some of the foundational practices of the church's history. It is less about reinventing the wheel and more about remembering where we came from and how to exercise muscles we let atrophy as we got a little too comfortable in the La-Z-Boy of church life as we've known it.

I hope this book asks questions that get you and your leadership team to rediscover your passion for discipleship ministry. The chapters are designed to be a practical guide, to give you nuts-and-bolts answers to how you can give your congregation the tools it needs to move toward a deeper and richer experience of what it means to follow Christ together. Discipleship doesn't happen by accident. But when it happens, churches, communities, and the world are changed.

It has been a blessing to hear the stories of congregations that have been putting these principles to work. The ideas and observations in this book have been the product of countless workshops and training sessions in which I have explored this pathway with church leaders and disciples at all stages of growth, and the results have been gratifying. I look forward to hearing about the way God works through this process with your congregation. I hope you share your story with us, too.

May your efforts be blessed and your work bear fruit,

Dr. Phil Maynard
July 2015

chapter one

Clarity

What do we really hope for as people become maturing disciples of Jesus Christ?

"Where there is no vision, the people perish."
—Proverbs 29:18 (KJV)

"Begin with the end in mind."
—Stephen Covey

From Membership to Discipleship

As I travel around the country, every gathering of church leaders I visit is wrestling with the same challenge. The form may differ, the buzz words may change, but the expectation is clear. We need to make a shift from making members to making disciples.

There are a variety of reasons for needing to make this shift. First and foremost is the faithful witness of the church. According to research by George Barna, nearly half of Americans claim to be "born again," but only about 13% reflect behaviors and attitudes that are different from the world around them. [1]

Consider the following graphic depicting the research of Barna: [2]

Is There a Discernable Difference?

Indicative Behaviors	Born-again Believer	Non-Believer
Loving	99%	95%
Compassionate	94%	95%
Donated to help others	47%	48%
Carry significant debt	33%	39%
Volunteered in community	29%	27%
Gave to homeless/poor	13%	12%
Corrected change error	19%	19%

According to George Barna in Growing True Disciples

My dear children, . . . I am again in the pains of childbirth until Christ is formed in you! (Galatians 4:19)

Can we at least agree that there should be a difference between the way Christians and non-believers engage their world?

There's a great video clip on YouTube of Francis Chan speaking at a Verge Conference. It is titled, "How Not to Make Disciples." In it, Francis pokes fun at the typical approach of the church to making disciples, describing an interaction with his daughter:

> I don't say to my daughter, "Rach, go clean your room," and have her come back in an hour and say, "Dad, I heard what you said. You said, 'Rachael, go clean your room.' I memorized it. I can say it in Greek. I am going to have a group of my friends come over and we're going to have a study about what it would be like if I cleaned my room.'" [3]

This highlights an additional reason we are struggling with actually making disciples. The church seems to have bought into the modern era philosophy that education would solve everything. If we could just teach our people more about the Bible and Jesus and Spiritual Disciplines and Issues Our World Faces, everything would be better. People would begin to behave and think and engage the world like Jesus did.

But the evidence suggests that we are not becoming more like Jesus.

As I visit and consult with congregational leaders all around the country and ask about their discipleship process, I usually get either a blank stare or a full-color brochure listing all the Bible studies and special interest studies being offered for that semester (note the academic language). There's nothing wrong with a strong Christian Education program. We need strong foundations on which to build. The problem is that we have replaced discipleship with Christian Education. They are not the same thing.

- Discipleship is not just about information. It is about behaviors.
- Discipleship is not just about education. It is about transformation.

A third reason the state of discipleship 'is what it is' is the direct result of misdirected focus in the larger church (e.g. denominations). The old adage "You get what you measure" is certainly at play in the church world, and what we measure is 'membership.' What we measure is 'worship attendance.' When we make an attempt at measuring discipleship, we naturally defer to convenience. We measure the 'number of persons in small discipling groups.' This, of course, doesn't really measure discipleship. It simply measures the persuasiveness of the church related to getting people into small groups. Typically, what is meant by a 'small discipling group' isn't even clearly articulated. You would think that after about 2,000 years of the church seeking to make disciples, we would have this down pat, yet it's clear that we don't.

Several years ago, while I was serving in the Florida Conference of the United Methodist Church as Director of Congregational Excellence, our Bishop held a Convocation. He brought together all the pastors and lay delegates from the hundreds of churches in the Conference for a time of sharing and visioning, and included in the laundry list of his priorities was an expectation that each and every congregation would be able to articulate an intentional process for making disciples of Jesus Christ. It was fascinating in the weeks that followed to track the number of people that contacted the Conference offices asking questions about how to follow up on this expectation. Some of the questions were for the kinds of clarification you might expect from people who were wanting to get their forms properly filled out: "We're not sure what the Bishop means by an 'intentional process' for making disciples. We offer *Disciple Bible Study.* Does that count?" I thought, "Well, sure, that's a great start, but it seems like there is so much more to building an intentional process."

One afternoon I answered my phone and got caught up in conversation with a very nice lady, who was a sincere and passionate long-time church leader and who was totally befuddled by this challenge. After 20 minutes, she got to the heart of the matter, the core of the dilemma on which I had been ruminating for a month, summed up in one succinct plea:

"We're just not sure what the Bishop means by *disciples*. We have *members* at our church. Are they the same thing?

Well, are they?

Don't leave a question like that hanging in the realm of the hypothetical: think about real individuals who are part of your congregation. I know a woman named Maria, whose face lights up with joy when she's in worship, who leads a GriefShare small group because as a widow she wants to help others find God's healing grace, who has a limited income yet gives sacrificially, who stretched beyond her comfort zone last year to shepherd kids in VBS, who studies her Bible daily, who regularly prays for others, and who witnesses to her neighbors by making them meals when they're sick. I also know a man, let's call him Mr. Grumbles, who attends church like clockwork on Sunday mornings, uses his pre-printed offering envelope every week, and helps two nights a month as one of the lock-the-church-building volunteers. He has more or less 'retired' from the rigors of spiritual growth, having achieved a reasonable plateau. And actually, I should write that he *used to* attend regularly. Recently, he was irritated that we preached once too often about welcoming all people (he thought our *all* was a little too *all*). In protest, he turned in his building key, stopped giving his $5.00 a week, and left us (albeit with a handwritten note explaining the proper interpretation of Scripture).

One of those people I just described is a disciple, and the other is a member (or former member), because the answer to the question of whether members and disciples are the same thing is, of course, "It all depends."

George Barna, in *Growing True Disciples*, offers a clear description of the marks of a true follower of Jesus:

- Disciples experience a changed future through their acceptance of Jesus Christ as Savior and of the Christian faith as their defining philosophy of life.

- Disciples undergo a changed lifestyle that is manifested through Christ-oriented values, goals, perspectives, activities, and relationships.

- Disciples mature into a changed worldview, attributable to a deeper comprehension of the true meaning and impact of Christianity. Truth becomes an entirely God-driven reality to a disciple. Pursuing the truths of God becomes the disciple's lifelong quest. [4]

Dallas Willard, in his book, *The Great Omission,* describes the process by which we detour from disciple-making to something less potent:

But in place of Christ's plan (making disciples), historical drift has substituted "Make converts (to a particular 'faith and practice') and baptize them into church membership." This causes two great omissions from the Great Commission to stand out. Most important, we start by omitting the making of disciples and enrolling people as Christ's students, when we should let all else wait for that. Then we also omit, of necessity, the step of taking our converts through training that will bring them ever-increasingly to do what Jesus directed. [5]

Members can be disciples and disciples can be members, but being a member does not automatically make one a growing, maturing disciple of Jesus Christ. The following chart depicts some of the distinctions that help illustrate the differences:

Members	Mature Disciples
Goal Get people to join the congregation.	**Goal** Create disciples who are increasing in their love of God and Neighbor.
Church Role Keep the members satisfied.	**Church Role** Provide opportunities and relationships to foster spiritual growth.
Leadership Role Encourage members to be involved in church activities.	**Leadership Role** Encourage disciples to grow in obedience to God and service to others.
Responsibility for Growth Church assumes primary responsibility for motivating people in their spiritual journey.	**Responsibility for Growth** Disciples assume primary responsibility for spiritual growth as the church provides opportunities and encouragement.

There are many other distinctions. What are some that come to mind for you based on your real world experience and your understanding of discipleship? (Note them in the box below.)

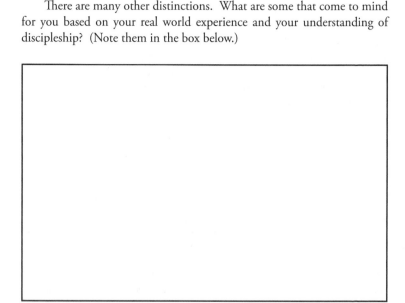

In my former job, I was part of the leadership that was supposed to be helping congregations figure these kinds of things out, but it became increasingly obvious from our ongoing conversations with church leaders that there really wasn't any clarity about answering even the most basic question, like, "Other than just knowing one when you see one, how do you spot a genuine disciple of Jesus Christ? What evidence are you actually looking for?"

So, we pulled together a group of pastors and key lay leadership from around the Conference and spent a day responding to these two foundational inquiries:

- What is a disciple?
- What does a disciple of Jesus Christ do?

At the end of the day, we had identified 153 things that a disciple is to be and do. Marker-covered newsprint adorned every wall in the room. Immediately, in a flash of uncommon wisdom, we figured out that it would be a bad idea to hand a new believer a list of over 150 things they were to be and do. That would probably send them running for the hills (or at least Florida's version of hills). But as we processed all that had been shared, three distinct themes emerged. We shaped these ideas into a definition that I have found greatly clarifies our hopes for people who commit to this journey of discipleship. These themes are reflected in the graphic below:

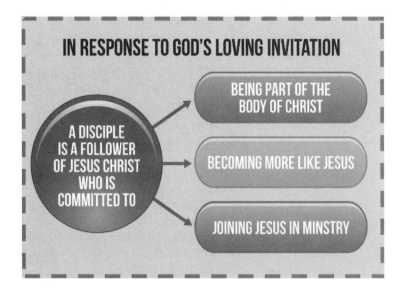

IN RESPONSE TO GOD'S LOVING INVITATION

A DISCIPLE IS A FOLLOWER OF JESUS CHRIST WHO IS COMMITTED TO

→ BEING PART OF THE BODY OF CHRIST

→ BECOMING MORE LIKE JESUS

→ JOINING JESUS IN MINSTRY

It is helpful to consider these themes through the lens of scripture, recalling the familiar words of Jesus in Matthew 4:19 (RSV):

> "***Follow me*** [being part of the body of Christ]
>
> *. . . **And I will make you*** [becoming more like Jesus]
>
> *. . . **Fishers of men*** [joining Jesus in ministry]."

Allow me to make some important observations:

- There are many different kinds of disciples at work in the world, but the discipleship characterized as being a follower of Jesus is unique. One may be a dedicated disciple of a very learned professor or a particular strand of philosophy. This means adhering to a set of ideas or ideals, but what we're talking about here is a lifestyle—a way of living—that emulates Jesus in every moment, in every action.

- Discipleship is a lifelong journey into the abundant life for which we were created. It is a process of continual development through which we grow in maturity (become Christ-centered and fully surrendered). In a culture obsessed with end results and perfection, it is crucial to remember that, for a disciple, it's the journey itself that is most important.

- Disciples are often described as 'learners,' but this is only one, potentially limited, understanding of discipleship. Discipleship in the biblical tradition is not just learning about Jesus, but becoming like Jesus—doing life as Jesus did life.

- The three dimensions of the life of a disciple (being part of the body of Christ, becoming more like Jesus, and joining Jesus in ministry) are broad strokes of commitment. Notice that they do not limit the options for the unique ways in which one may engage the body of Christ. They do not constrict the options for how one grows to become like Jesus or even dictate how one must be partnered in ministry. They only point to the reality that discipleship is inclusive of all three of these dimensions of growth. Each disciple must personally discover how God has 'wired' them and is calling them to be engaged. There is no 'one size fits all' for discipleship.

The Jesus of the gospels is our guide. The words and actions of Jesus present a clear model for making choices that lead us more deeply into **being** part of the body of Christ, **becoming** more like Jesus, and **joining** Jesus in ministry. And when talking about this definition of discipleship, I like to add the words "for life" after "follower of Jesus Christ," because we never retire from being a disciple, even though we all know of people who have pitched their beach chair on the ministry shore and are enjoying a nice, long nap.

The three categories of engagement that this lifelong, growth-oriented disciple commits to are intentionally broad. For example, there are many valid ways a person can commit to **Being Part of the Body of Christ**:

✓ Participating in corporate worship.

✓ Being part of a small group.

✓ Participating in a Bible study.

✓ Engaging in a partnership with another believer.

✓ Serving other people.

Some churches are even enthusiastically embracing technology to expand the reach of the body of Christ. In these congregations, you might find yourself:

✓ Joining a 'live-stream' of a worship service.
✓ Participating in a video-conference conversation focusing on spiritual disciplines.
✓ Texting someone in need with a notification that you and your church are praying for them.

Of course, technology moves so fast—unlike most churches—that by the time this book reaches publication, these examples might already have been cast aside in favor of the latest communications trend. Even so, you get the point.

Similarly, **Becoming More Like Jesus** can take several forms. For example:

✓ Studying the Word of God (the Scriptures).
✓ Acting in mercy.
✓ Praying.
✓ Supporting one another.
✓ Practicing means of grace.
✓ Partnering with other believers.

Joining Jesus in Ministry to the world might include things like:

✓ Random acts of kindness.
✓ Serving on a mission team.
✓ Supporting a community service organization.
✓ Sharing our resources with those in need.

The possibilities are endless. To reiterate, there is no such thing as 'discipleship-in-a-box'! Discipleship is a very personal journey, and what works for one person will not necessarily work for another. The key is to be inclusive rather than exclusive. The goal is not to fit people into our pre-conceived category or ministry slot but to help them discover how God is calling them to grow into a life of being a committed disciple of Jesus. By being creatively adaptable, we have greater success in helping others take the leap to try out a ministry or spiritual growth opportunity. And once they've taken that initial step, their new experience can spark a passion for a deeper connection that leads to engagement in other areas.

It's not a direct-line process like learning welding at the local vo-tech school. It's fluid and multi-track, and different for every 'student.' And each of the themes we've described can be further understood as having distinctive dimensions of practical spiritual life skill sets that correspond with them.

Being Part of the Body of Christ

Being Part of the Body of Christ includes both a **Life of Worship** and **a Life of Hospitality.** **A Life of Worship** means participation in corporate worship, but it also includes personal worship (e.g. a devotional time) and eventually an entire lifestyle of worship where every action and circumstance becomes an opportunity to give glory to God.

I love good worship—any style will do—where I am meaningfully invited into the presence of Christ and challenged to take clear next steps on my journey of discipleship. However, in my reading of Scripture, the focus is not on getting people to a weekly gathering with great music and inspirational messages. Don't get me wrong. Those things still hold great value, but the calling of Scripture is to a lifestyle of worship—how can I honor and connect to God moment by moment, and how can I practice the sacrificial giving of myself and my resources to those in need?

Consider the following everyday examples:

- As I walk down the street I meet Sam coming from the other direction. From past experience I know Sam tends to be a little needy, and I don't really have time for an extended conversation at the moment. How I interact with Sam is either an opportunity to bring glory to God or not.

- Later that same afternoon, I am faced with a choice about how to use the financial resources God has provided. I can either buy new patio furniture or support a ministry I admire that is building an orphanage. The choice I make is an opportunity to either bring glory to God or glory to my patio.

Eugene Peterson captures this call to a lifestyle of worship in *The Message* version of Romans 12:1:

So here's what I want you to do, God helping you: Take your every-
day, ordinary life—your sleeping, eating, going-to-work, and walk-
ing-around life—and place it before God as an offering.

A Life of Hospitality includes the traditional roles of being part of
the church community and welcoming new people to worship, but it also
includes our personal relationships with (and our acceptance of) people
who are outside the church and quite unlike us, even to the point of intentionally building relationships with persons beyond the church in order to
embody Christ's love for them.

Often when we think about hospitality, it is in the context of how we
welcome people when they come as guests to our worship services. But this
is just a very small portion of a life of Christ-centered hospitality. I think of
hospitality as having four distinct dimensions:

- Interpersonal.
- Intentional.
- Invitational.
- Incarnational.

Undergirding each of these individual dimensions of hospitality are two
additional sub-layers. Each of the four dimensions of hospitality is experienced in both a corporate and a personal sense. For example, **Interpersonal**
hospitality from a corporate perspective is all about the opportunities we
create for developing authentic relationships within our home congregation. Meanwhile, from a personal perspective, interpersonal hospitality has
to do with our practice of forgiveness of those who have wronged us in
some way, our acceptance of those who are different from us, and even our
willingness to be held accountable to our call as a disciple.

Intentional hospitality from a personal perspective is practiced as we engage those we do not know or do not know well, helping them to feel
welcome in the body of Christ and leaving them with a sense that this
community is a place where they will fit in. From a corporate perspective,
intentional hospitality is the mindfulness with which we engage guests and
provide space and opportunity for building relationships.

Invitational hospitality is living into our vow to be faithful witnesses as we
invite others to discover Jesus through the activities and relationships of our
community of faith. As practiced by a congregation, it encompasses the

opportunities we provide for building connections and the tools to resource persons in issuing such invitations.

Incarnational hospitality—a goal for the life of every mature disciple—is how we intentionally build deeper relationships with people outside of the church so that we may be an expression of the love of Christ in their lives. The goal is not necessarily to get them to church (although this may be a natural byproduct of the relationship), but to get them to Jesus. Hospitality is not about hidden agendas, but about helping people discover God's love for them. Part of the role of the church (the corporate part of incarnational hospitality) is to equip, resource, and celebrate the building of these relationships.

The research is clear. Some 60-80% of people who walk through a church door step inside because they were invited by someone with whom they have an existing relationship. The draw is not the church itself. Much like the first century, the culture in which we live is not sure there is much about the church that is relevant to their lives. In different words, but with the same disregard, we hear the world say, "*Can anything good come from Nazareth?*" (John 1:46) But we often have opportunities, like Philip inviting Nathanael to come see what God is doing, to convince people to meet Jesus on the strength of their relationship with us.

They trust the person, not the institution.

Becoming More Like Jesus

Becoming more like Jesus, we live a **Life Opening to Jesus** and **A Life Obeying Jesus.** **A Life Opening to Jesus** points us in the direction of spiritual practices, such as scriptural engagement and prayer, which help us develop an awareness of the presence of Christ.

Dallas Willard, in *The Divine Conspiracy,* writes:

So when Jesus directs us to pray, "Thy kingdom come," he does not mean we pray for it to come into existence. Rather, we pray for it to take over at all points in the personal, social, and political order where it is now excluded. . . .

Jesus came among us to show and teach the life for which we were made. He came very gently, opened access to the governance of God with him, and set afoot a conspiracy of freedom in truth among human beings. Having overcome death he remains among us. By relying on his word and presence we are enabled to reintegrate the little realm that makes up our life into the infinite rule of God. And that is the eternal kind of life . . . making us part of his life and him a part of ours. [6]

This dimension of discipleship is really focused on helping us to develop an awareness of God's grace at work in our world and to place us in a position to receive and respond to that grace, that working of the Spirit. It is a surprise to many people, even some within the church, that Jesus, through the Holy Spirit, is present and active in our world even when we are unaware of this presence and activity. I think that one of the most exciting benefits of the practice of spiritual disciplines is that of developing our awareness of this constant working of the Spirit.

When I first started teaching about discipleship, I called this dimension "A Life Formed by Scripture." Of course, Scripture has always been central to the Christian experience, and we most often encounter it through playing our proper roles as teachers and students as we study and reflect on passages and try to learn the skills for discerning what the Word wants to speak into our lives. As an 'expert' on discipleship, I stressed the important work of getting people into the Scriptures, but this never really captured the essence of what I wanted to communicate. Then one day I had a brainstorm. I realized that grace was the answer! What I really wanted to communicate was connecting with God's grace! So then I entitled this dimension "A Life Formed by Grace."

I thought it was a brilliant solution. After all, I come from a Wesleyan background, and central to that understanding are the Means of Grace. But when I started teaching about these dimensions in local churches, I soon discovered that even good Methodists didn't seem to get the concept. (Evidently we are not doing a great job at helping our Methodist disciples develop these spiritual practices that are directly connected to their denominational heritage.) So, eventually I settled on calling it "A Life Opening to Jesus," because that's what spiritual practices do—they open us to Jesus. They help us develop an awareness of God's presence and activity.

- There is the role of **intimacy**, as we engage in practices of prayer and build our relationship with God.
- There is the role of **submission**, where we learn to remove ourselves from the focus of our personal viewpoint.
- There is the role of **obedience**, where we form our lives around the teaching of Scripture.

For me, developing our awareness of God's presence and energetic activity in the world around us is a highlight. Consider the spiritual practice of serving. For many years I have been taking mission teams to Jamaica to support a variety of projects ranging from free medical clinics to Vacation Bible Schools, from construction to evangelism. It is common during preparation for such a trip that participants on a team will talk about the blessing they are going to be for the people to whom they will minister. The conversation on the way home, however, is always very different in tone.

On my last trip to Jamaica, one of the participants was new to mission trips and had never been out of the United States. As we prepared for the trip, she talked constantly about her gratitude that the Lord was allowing her to use her abundance of material blessings and spiritual education to bring hope to "those poor people in Jamaica in their ramshackle houses." She thanked God for the chance to "help them see Jesus." But when she returned and shared her story with her home congregation, it had morphed into this: "I was so blessed by the people who allowed us to come into their homes and their lives. I thought I knew what it was to have faith, but seeing that community that we casually judge by our standards as having nothing . . . seeing the joy they shared and their commitment to helping one another . . . I have a whole new appreciation for what it means to love Jesus."

Or consider the power of study and reflection to open us up to experience Jesus in fresh ways. One of my favorite devotional activities is to read from the saints and spiritual leaders of the church through the ages. Through their wisdom and the stories of their spiritual journeys, I am becoming more and more aware of the ways God is at work in my own life and our present world. Take the story of St. Francis of Assisi. Though Francis lived some 800 years ago, his struggle between material comforts and selfish living versus a commitment to the poor and a focus on godly priorities is perhaps even more relevant in this age of income disparity and wealth versus poverty (see the discussion on Affluenza a little later on in this chapter). Francis' love of the created world and his deep connection to all living things also resonates with profound relevance in this era of environmental degradation.

Or consider how engaging regularly with small groups for study and prayer can transform us in ways that no individual habits or large group gathering can. Many congregations have some form of small group experience. Those who do this well move beyond the classroom model to a Christian Conferencing approach (a term coined by the Wesleyan movement). This is a robust small group strategy for sharing our faith, supporting one another in the journey, and challenging one another to growth toward maturity. One of the great benefits of this approach is the awareness of the presence and activity of God that develops as we share our individual stories and experiences.

A Life Obeying Jesus begins with our acceptance of a relationship with Jesus and our commitment to becoming like Jesus. As we move toward maturity, we begin to apply the teachings of Scripture to our own lives, and we develop partnerships with others to help them grow as disciples. Some of us grew up in a church culture that made obedience to Jesus sound just like a bunch of rules to follow if we were going to be 'good' Christians. This little ditty, recounted in the *Dictionary of Christianese*, comes to mind:

> [D]on't drink, smoke, or chew . . . don't dance, drink, smoke, or chew . . . don't cuss (or swear), dance, drink, smoke, or chew. . . . Often the rhythm and meter of the slogan are deliberately structured so that the word chew rhymes with the word do. For example: "I don't drink, and I don't chew; and I don't go with girls who do." The slogan is associated with Baptists, fundamentalists, evangelicals, and other conservative Christians. [7]

There is still a strong carryover into our current church culture, especially in more conservative traditions. I was at dinner with my brother-in-law a while back—a staunch Baptist. He opted for ice water instead of a nice glass of wine at the Italian restaurant, explaining that he was a Baptist dining out in public in his hometown. The implication, of course, was that things might have been different if we were in Las Vegas (where whatever happens stays in the strictest confidence, at least if you believe the marketing). But obeying Jesus is not about adhering to a list of rules—home or away. The focus of **A Life Obeying Jesus** is at its heart about discovering the abundance of life, the eternal life, offered by Jesus and gleaned from reflecting on the Scriptures and the applicability of eternal scriptural truths to our daily lives.

As the psalmist writes:

> *Blessed are those . . .*
> *Who delight in the law of the Lord*
> *And meditate on his law day and night.*

They are like a tree planted by streams of water,
Which yields its fruit in season
And whose leaf does not wither—
Whatever they do prospers . . .

For the Lord watches over the way of the righteous. . . .

—Psalm 1 (NRSV)

From financial planning to building strong relationships, from spiritual practices to how to deal with conflict, from organizational development to lives of compassion, the Scriptures point us to the fullness of the life God has in store for us. Our responsibility is to discover that life and help others do the same.

Joining Jesus in Ministry

Joining Jesus in Ministry to the world means that we embrace **A Life of Service** and **A Life of Generosity.** **A Life of Service** includes supporting the ministry of the local church with our time and energy, and participating in service projects sponsored by the church, but it also includes a lifestyle investing the best of who we are in service to others.

It has been said many times and many ways—sorry for the Christmas song reference—that if you want people to grow, get them to serve. There is much evidence to back this up. Have you ever wondered why every youth group you know about does a mission trip somewhere away from home? Why do that? Shouldn't the real job of the youth ministry be to help our kids be more 'spiritual'? The answer is that youth pastors have discovered a basic spiritual truth: if you want people to grow, get them to serve. (And if you want to get them excited about trying out this lifestyle of service, take them someplace a little more exotic than their own backyard where they can't help but come away with a wholly different perspective.)

My calling to ministry was clearly to serve as a pastor in a local church setting. I was very focused on discipleship and spiritual formation. In fact, I stayed and did a program beyond the M.Div. to focus on Wesleyan spiritual formation. But I also learned a huge practical lesson about ministry in my very first year in seminary. It has transformed the way I approached ministry for the next 20 years.

I was invited by a mission group doing work through a medical clinic in Haiti to use my skills from my first career in radiologic sciences (I had taught radiologic sciences at the University of Central Florida prior to entering the ministry). The mission group needed a radiographer to go to the clinic and set up x-ray equipment and a dark room, then train local support to do some simple procedures. It was a great experience. I got the equipment working, darkroom built, and did some training. I also got about $20,000 worth of supplies donated to the clinic from local hospitals.

I was so moved by the impact of the work there, that when I came back I was seriously considering becoming a full-time missionary. Then a very wise pastor helped me see that great opportunities to serve and make a difference weren't limited to international locales. They were all around me, embedded in the fabric of my home community, particularly in the possibilities uniquely available to me for leading congregations so they could inspire and equip hearts committed to making a difference. I was very grateful for the insight and for seeing the opportunity God had granted me. It changed the way I have done ministry over my career.

A Life of Generosity includes presenting our tithes and offerings as an act of worship, but it also includes creating a lifestyle with margins that allows us to respond to the needs of others God puts in our path on a daily basis. This dimension of our discipleship helps us to live into the covenant created between God and God's people way back in history, all the way to the time of Abram (later called Abraham). We are blessed to be a blessing.

> *I will make you into a great nation,*
> *And I will bless you;*
> *I will make your name great,*
> *And you will be a blessing.*

—Genesis 12:2-3 (NRSV)

In a culture plagued by Affluenza (the need for more stuff we don't need, purchased with money we don't have), the idea of creating a lifestyle of generosity is a challenge. Even pastors fall prey to this!

A few years ago I was offered a supplemental quarter-time position with the United Methodist General Board of Discipleship (now Discipleship Ministries) in New Church Starts. My response upon receiving the first paycheck was to consider all the things we could do with that extra money. Through this extra income, God had provided the resources needed to support the mission work I was involved with in Jamaica, but all I could think about was the cool stuff I could do with the bonus loot. It's a common affliction. **A Life of Generosity** helps us think differently about the resources with which we have been entrusted.

Holy Expectations

The following graphic puts all six dimensions of discipleship we have just discussed into an image that brings to mind the petals of a flower. I call it the daisy diagram. That's because it reminds of the way young girls (at least in the pre-digital entertainment days when many of us grew up) would pull the petals off a daisy, repeating the words, "He loves me, he loves me not." I want to suggest that these petals in the diagram are all "we love Jesus" petals. Each of them reflects a dimension of our lives as a disciple, and each one of them is as equally important as every other.

Just like the 'fruit' of the Spirit

The Apostle Paul didn't call them the 'fruits' of the Spirit. That could be taken to mean that we could pick and choose which fruit we want the Spirit to exhibit in our lives. Paul called them fruit, a collective noun. They are collectively the natural product of the working of the Spirit in our lives. I think the same is true for these dimensions of discipleship. They all reflect our love for Jesus. We don't get to pick and choose which of them are developed in our lives.

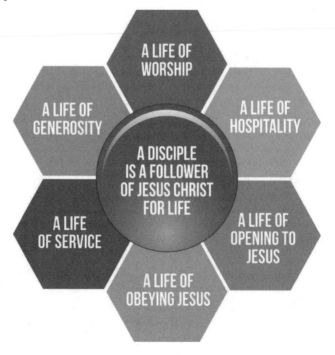

The Scriptures are clear. The Great Commission is clear. The church exists to make disciples of Jesus Christ. Jesus said,

> *"Therefore, go [literally translated: 'as you go'] and make disciples of all nations [literally translated: 'people groups'], baptizing them in the name of the Father and of the Son and of the Holy Spirit, and teaching them to obey everything I have commanded you."*
>
> —Matthew 28:19-20 (NIV)

All the Bible scholars reading this know that whenever there is a 'therefore' in Scripture, we had better stop and find out what it is there for. In this case, it reminds us:

> *"All authority in heaven and on earth has been given to me [Jesus]."*
>
> —Matthew 28:18 (NIV)

Jesus has the authority and we have the calling to do one thing: **make disciples**. The first step in answering this holy summons is to be clear about what happens next for those joining us in this journey with Jesus. What hopes does God have for their lives as they become committed followers who belong to the body of Christ? What does it really mean to become more like Jesus? What will be the cost to authentically join Jesus and his disciples in ministry to the world?

Consider the following illustration taken from my book, *Shift: Helping Congregations Back Into the Game of Effective Ministry:*

> Jim and Sally were looking for a way to get connected in their new community. On Sunday morning they decided to start checking out the local churches. They visited Grace Church and really liked both the music and the pastor's message. At the end of the service an invitation was given. People could make a commitment to Jesus or renew their commitment to Jesus or, if they were ready, they could come forward and join the church.
>
> Jim and Sally looked at each other and nodded. Then they walked up the aisle and became members of the congregation, giving their names to the pastor and saying yes to the stated vows. [8]

In a church culture where the number of people on the rolls is the most important thing, this scenario might make sense. But it might also explain why, in a large percentage of our congregations, only 25–40% of the membership actually attends worship in a given month or why so few people say that the church is actually relevant in their lives or why congregations become focused on taking care of 'their own,' rather than transforming their communities.

Of course most of our congregations don't just extend an open invitation like the one described above (although I have seen it done). We expect people to attend a 'membership' class before they can join. Most commonly, this class runs between 2–4 hours and includes the following:

- An introduction to the pastor, staff, and key leaders.
- An overview of the ministries of the church and explanation of how the church can serve those becoming members.
- A brief history of the congregation/church.
- An introduction to the history of the denomination with core beliefs.
- And (of course) . . . a pledge card for financial commitments.

Again, in a church culture where it's all about getting people involved in the local church and keeping people happy in the local church, this makes sense. This is a scenario being lived out in congregations all across the country. Our membership emphasis has become more about joining and feeling at home in our club, rather than expecting and helping members to grow as disciples of Jesus.

In the last church I served as a 'real' pastor before taking a position on Conference staff, we addressed this setting of expectations through the use of a Membership Covenant. The leadership team decided that just using the traditional vows for membership was not enough—it did not bring enough clarity. Coming from the United Methodist tradition, those vows read:

I will support the Church by my prayers, presence, gifts, service, and witness.

Building from that foundation, we developed the following covenant expectations to bring more clarity to the process:

Traditional Vows	Dimensions of Discipleship	Membership Covenant
Prayers	Opening to Jesus/ Obeying Jesus	Participate regularly in a small discipleship group or other accountable discipling relationship.
Presence	A Life of Worship	Participate in weekly worship at least 3 weekends each month unless prveted by illness or travel.
Gifts	A Life of Generosity	Commit to proportional giving to the ministries of this congregation and to moving toward a tithe.
Service	A Life of Service	Serve in some way in the local community (beyond the walls of the church) each month.
Witness	A Life of Hospitality	Invite someone to come with me to church/events at least tree times per year and build at least three relationships outside the church to wtness the love of Christ.

Since a covenant has two sides, it was equally important to be clear about the church's commitments in this relationship.

Traditional Vows	Dimensions of Discipleship	Commitment of the Church
Prayers	A Life Opening to Jesus/Obeying Jesus	Provide a variety of discipling relationships, including small groups, mentors, discipleship coaching, spiritual direction. Instruction in all dimensions of discipleship.
Presence	A Life of Worship	Provide passionate worship experiences done with excellence.
Gifts	A Life of Generosity	Provide training in biblical financial management and multiple ways to contribute to our ministries.
Service	A Life of Service	Assistance in discovering how disciples are gifted for service and multiple opportunities to explore personal service 'fit.'
Witness	A Life of Hospitality	Support in invitational hospitality by resourcing materials and training in relational evangelism and faith sharing.

When the covenant agreement was first developed, the leadership team made a commitment to live into the covenant for a year before introducing it to the congregation. At the end of the year, members of the leadership team shared their testimonies, and the covenant was introduced.

In January, following a tradition of offering a Wesleyan Covenant Renewal Service each year, the Membership Covenant was offered as an option for current members to sign. Of course, not all of them did, and we continued to minister to the non-signers just exactly as we always had. After all, they had joined up under a different set of expectations, and it was important to honor that relationship.

However, the Membership Covenant soon became the new standard for membership in that congregation. We moved away from a model of placing a high value on people becoming 'members.' We emphasized that those who had decided to join our band of disciples were expected to understand that the journey ahead and the work at hand was not all about them. Their commitment would be to actively involve themselves in a congregation that was making a difference in the community by changing people's lives.

To be clear, not all people who were currently members signed on to the new covenant, and not all people who were considering membership decided to embrace that level of commitment. I remember one middle-aged woman who came up to me distraught after a new member class and said, "What if I'm not ready to do this?" She had tears in her eyes, so deep and honest was her struggle. So, I comfortingly responded, "No problem. You've been worshiping with us for five years now. During that time, you've been invited be a part of small group experiences. Nobody has ever asked you for a membership card to attend an event or fellowship dinner. I visited you when you were in the hospital, and I even baptized your granddaughter. None of that changes. No membership required. When you're ready to become part of a team making a difference in this community, let us know and we'll get you signed up."

Churches all across the country are moving in this direction to bring clarity to exactly what they mean when they remind their congregants that they are called to be growing as disciples. Here are a couple of examples: [9]

Membership Covenant

I, _____, trusting Jesus Christ as my Lord and Savior, seeking to be led by the Holy Spirit, and being in agreement with the mission and vision of Evergreen Church, as a part of the United Methodist Church, now desire to unite with the Evergreen Church family. In doing so, I commit myself to God and to the other members to do the following:

*As we **experience** God, I will strengthen the integrity of my church*

> *...by lovingly pursuing important personal relationships with other members (1 Peter 1:22)*

> *...by refusing to participate in gossip or other negative conversation (Ephesians 4:29)*

> *...by actively encouraging participation in Home Groups (Acts 2:42, 46)*

> *...by living a godly life in response to God's grace (Micah 6:8; 1 John 2:6)*

*As we **exalt** God, I will share in the joyful responsibility of my church*

> *...by attending faithfully with a heart ready for sincere worship (Hebrews 10:25)*

> *...by being open-minded in worship, more committed to Spirit & truth than to comfort & tradition (John 4:23)*

> *...by warmly welcoming those who visit (Romans 15:7)*

> *...by praying for its faithfulness and growth (1 Samuel 12:23; 1 Thessalonians 1:1-*

*As we **extend** God to others, I will serve Christ in the world through the ministry of my church*

> *...by discovering my gifts and talents (1 Peter 4:10) and being equipped to serve others (Ephesians 4)*

> *...by seeking to have and live from a servant's heart (Philippians 2:3-7)*

> *...by giving regularly to God through the church (Leviticus 27:30; 1 Corinthians 16:2)*

> *...by inviting those without a church to attend worship with me (Luke 14:23)*

New members of Medina United Methodist Church are expected to actively pursue a personal relationship with Jesus Christ. By fulfilling the membership expectations, you should be on a good pathway to becoming a disciple of Christ. [10]

Traditional Vows	Dimensions of Discipleship	Membership Expectations
Prayers Galatians 2:20 Ephesians 4:14-15 Matthew 4:19	**A Life Open to Jesus A Life Obeying Jesus** (Intentional Faith Development)	Participate regularly in a small group study, Bible class, or ministry team that encourages spiritual growth. Engage in a personal Bible study for prayer/reflection.
Presence Romans 12:1	**A Life of Worship** (Passionate Worship)	Participate in weekly worship unless prevented by illness or travel.
Gifts Proverbs 22:9 Acts 20:35	**A Life of Generosity** (Extravagant Generosity)	Commit to proportional giving to the ministries of this congregation and to moving toward a tithe and beyond.
Service Matthew 25:44-45	**A Life of Service** (Risk Taking Mission)	Serve in some ongoing way in the local community. Serve in some ongoing way within the church (e.g., usher, committee member, Sunday School teacher).
Witness John 15:12	**A Life of Hospitality** (Radical Hospitality)	Build relationships outside the church to witness the love of Christ and invite someone to attend worship services or church events at least three times per year. Attempt to meet and greet a different member of MUMC at each worship service you attend.

New members can expect MUMC to provide opportunities for growth toward a Christ-Centered life.

Traditional Vows	Dimensions of Discipleship	MUMC Opportunities
Prayers	**A life Open to Jesus** **A life Obeying Jesus** (Intentional Faith Development)	We will teach you how to become a maturing disciple of Christ through spiritual practices, Bible studies, classes, and other faith development opportunities.
Presence	**A Life of Worship** (Passionate Worship)	We invite you to participate in Holy Communion and all worship services. We provide baptism, wedding, and funeral services upon request.
Gifts	**A Life of Generosity** (Extravagant Generosity)	We will teach you the benefits of a giving heart and to exercise Biblical principles of stewardship.
Service	**A Life of Service** (Risk Taking Mission)	We will help you discover your spiritual gifts and how they may be used in ministry and mission opportunities.
Witness	**A Life of Hospitality** (Radical Hospitality)	We offer fellowship and faith sharing opportunities. We provide visitation ministry, prayer ministry, and pastoral counseling.

Signature: _____   Date:_____

_____

The Gallup organization, reporting research done with faith communities in *Growing An Engaged Church,* notes:

> Members need to know what is expected of them if they are to develop a strong sense of belonging within their congregation. Clarifying expectations creates a sense of stability, assuring members that they are valued. . . . 'A clear set of expectations' is one of the ways members know they are receiving something of value from their congregation. . . .
>
> So the very first thing you, as leaders, must do to ensure congregational effectiveness is to clarify membership expectations. What do you want your members' lives to look like—what is the fruit they should bear as a result of being planted in the soil of your church? What kinds of behaviors are consistent with being a member of your church? Do you want your members to be involved in community service projects? What about frequency of attendance? Should your members be involved in some kind of study, growth, or support group? What do you expect in terms of financial support. . . ?
>
> These are all questions you can answer by laying out clear membership expectations. Clear expectations lay the foundation for everything else your congregation is called to do and be. Without them, members will drift—eventually, right out the door. [11]

Beginning with the End in Mind

This admonition from Stephen Covey in his classic text, *The 7 Habits of Highly Effective People,* is good advice for congregations that hope to make growing, maturing disciples of Jesus Christ. We need to be clear about what we hope for people as they partner with us on the journey of discipleship, and we need to be equally clear about what they can expect from us to support them on the journey.

Consider the following as a starting point for casting a vision for maturing discipleship:

Maturing disciples . . .

- Live lives honoring God in the ways they work, play, and engage others.
- Intentionally build relationships in order to be Christ to someone.
- Take responsibility for their own spiritual growth.
- Disciple someone else, helping them move toward maturity.
- Use their gifts and talents to serve others.
- Live within margins in order to bless others more.

Questions for Reflection

1. How does your congregation define "discipleship"?

2. What do you measure to determine the "success" of your discipleship ministry?

3. What would be needed in your context to transition from a focus on Christian Education to a focus on discipleship?

4. As you consider the six dimensions of discipleship described in this chapter, what are the areas for which you:

- Have strong training elements in place?

- Can identify gaps in your training process?

5. In what ways does your congregation clearly articulate "hopes" for those partnering with you in the discipleship journey?

6. If a guest asked you, "What is your vision for me as a disciple of Jesus Christ?" how would you respond?

chapter two

Movements

How people grow toward maturity
as disciples of Jesus Christ
AND
What people say they need from the church to
grow toward maturity as disciples
of Jesus Christ

"A disciple is not greater than his teacher, but everyone when fully trained will be like his teacher." –Luke 6:40

"The ultimate goal of all of this is transformed lives." –Phil Maynard

Discipleship as a Journey

I am a grandfather now. Just as it was a joy to watch my own children move through the early phases of life and become responsible adults making their way in the world, it is a reprise and refinement of that joy to watch my grandkids go through the same stages (and without the pressure of having to be the primary caregiver). As I watched the grandkids learn to walk, then read, then clean their own rooms (sort of), then drive, I took joy in their triumphs and comfort in the wisdom that their missteps would only be temporary and would ultimately make them stronger as fully functional humans.

For those of us who've been disciples for a long time, we experience a similar sense of pride (and sometimes anxiety) as we watch new Christians move through the phases of growth in their relationship with Jesus. We know we are not called to maintain the status quo as babes in the faith. The Apostle Paul urges us to grow into maturity or completeness. John Wesley uses the language of "Christian Perfection."

We are not meant to remain as children . . . but we are meant to speak the truth in love, and to grow up in every way into Christ, the head.

—Ephesians 4:14 (J.B. Phillips)

Whichever way we look at it, from the very beginning, discipleship has been a journey toward the fullness of life that is offered to us in Jesus Christ. This journey happens in stages of development very similar to our life stages. In fact, this is the very language that Tim Putman uses in his book, *Real Life Discipleship*:

- Pre-stage (not yet "born again").
- Infancy.
- Childhood.
- Adolescent/Young Adult.
- Parenthood/Adult. [1]

It doesn't take a lot of imagination to see the parallels to the journey in faith. In infancy, we are exploring everything. I remember my granddaughter, Angel, as she lurched around the room, mastering her first steps, picking up everything she could get her little hands on and inevitably sticking whatever it was in her mouth! The whole world is new, and we're amazed by what we're experiencing. But we don't really have a useful role in that world except for our featured performance to be adorably cute and cuddly for the adults around us. Consider some of the distinguishing characteristics in the life of an infant:

- Don't know anything about their world.
- Completely dependent upon someone more mature.
- Have to be fed, changed, held, comforted, and carried.
- Time of greatest discovery.

In the childhood phase we are all about learning our world, and we're insatiable. I remember Angel crawling up into my lap, dragging *Goodnight Moon* behind her. She wanted to hear every word again and again, even before she understood what words really were. We don't know much, if anything, about the world at that stage, and someone has to guide us along, teach us how to navigate it, keep us from doing things that will hurt us, and help us to develop in ways that will be the foundations for the rest of life.

Consider some of the characteristics representing the life of a child:

- Learning the language.
- Learning basic skills—eating, getting dressed, feeding themselves.
- Learning how to live in relationship with others—parents, friends, teachers.
- Living within very clear boundaries set by adults.
- Still being very dependent upon more mature persons.
- Learning things by trying them—e.g. touching a hot stove and discovering it will burn.

The adolescent phase moves us into taking responsibility for our lives. We begin to establish some independence. We discover what works well for us. We make some of our own decisions about how to do life. I remember Angel struggling with her selection of high school classes (calculus or easy math?) and wrestling with the choice of extra-curricular activities (softball or marching band?). They were her choices to make, but she still relied heavily on the advice of the adults around her.

Consider some of the characteristics representing the life of an adolescent:

- Beginning to assert independence.
- Finding a sense of place in life.
- Developing their own ways of doing things.
- Pushing boundaries.
- Being heavily influenced by peers.
- Determining their own future.

Up to this point in the development process, everything has been about us (the *me*). As we move into adulthood/parenthood, however, a major shift occurs. For the first time in our development it is about someone else—not just us. We have responsibilities beyond ourselves and our own personal priorities. Traveling back mentally to the months before Angel was born, I can remember the dramatic shift in perspective on the part of my son, Josh. Rather than figuring out how he was going to be able to afford that new tricked-out Ford Mustang he had been eyeballing, it suddenly dawned on him that perhaps he should save his money for financing the impending mass purchase of diapers—or, heaven forbid, starting a college savings fund. The parenthood/adult phase moves us squarely into the realm of focusing beyond ourselves. We realize that life done well involves helping others do life well. We continue to grow personally, but the focus becomes other-centered.

This is why the stages that are useful in describing the physical growth of human beings are also so helpful in describing their spiritual progress. For the purposes of describing the phases of growth as a disciple, I like to use the terms **Searching, Exploring, Beginning, Growing,** and **Maturing**:

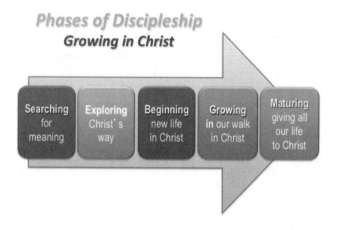

Searching *(pre-life in Christ)*: We all seek to make sense of our lives, asking questions like "What gives my life purpose, joy, and fulfillment?" We may seek to fill this fundamental need many different ways. (See Acts 17:22.)

Exploring *(infancy)*: We may attend church and want to belong, but have not yet committed to following Jesus. We may wrestle intellectually with God's presence in our life, often with more caution than curiosity. The longer we attend without an official 'joining', however, the less likely we are to formally commit. (See John 1:45.)

Beginning *(childhood)*: We are beginning to understand and put into practice our newfound faith. Growth can be awkward. We are often vulnerable to insecurity and doubt. We are also the most excited about our faith at this stage. This is the largest and most active segment of congregants involved in church activities. (See Matthew 7:22-24.)

Growing *(adolescence):* We are eager to be identified as Christians and are going public with our faith. We are increasingly willing to take personal responsibility for our growing relationship with Jesus. We seek to integrate our faith into life in a holistic way and look to Jesus to help us live our life. (See Ephesians 4:14.)

Maturing *(parents):* We are moving toward complete surrender of our lives to Jesus. We exist to know, love, obey, serve, and be with Jesus. We also realize that the role of a disciple is to help make other disciples, and we live with that focus. (See Galatians 2:20.)

It is important to note here that not only does development happen in **phases** and that the different people in our congregations will find themselves in different phases, but that the various **dimensions** of the life of a disciple will often reflect differing levels of maturity. For example, a person may have a great passion for serving others and a well-developed sense of calling (those would be characteristics associated with the 'growing' phase of the service dimension in our handy chart). But despite this person's advanced status in the service phase, they may simultaneously be only in the 'beginning' phase for opening to Jesus. They may have expressed their intention to develop the spiritual disciplines that will deepen their connection to Jesus, but they might not yet have moved into a status that could be described as a 'growing' relationship in that area. Churches frequently see this scenario of unbalanced growth, particularly the imbalance between service and opening to Jesus, because opening to Jesus can be unfamiliar terrain, while the idea of service is so intuitive and easily accessible for so many people who feel the urging of the Holy Spirit. The good news is that the service dimension can serve as an important catalyst for growth in other areas.

This is natural and good, but leads to confusion in growing disciples if they (and their leaders and mentors) don't have a clear understanding of the different dimensions of discipleship and phases of growth within each.

Phases, Characteristics, Dimensions

A friend of mine, Jack, is an American contractor who lives overseas, where he runs a construction business. Jack and I got connected through a seemingly obscure relationship with a mission organization (ReGenesis Ministries) for which I provide leadership. Jack is what one might describe as "a little rough around the edges" (okay, maybe a lot). He is a lapsed Catholic and former drug addict.

Yet, each time I take a mission team to that area, Jack takes the week off from his business and arranges supplies for the project, provides equipment for the team, and even trains the team for the needs of the project. During those team experiences, Jack also goes to church, attends daily devotional times, makes sure that we pray at every meal, and announces to everybody we meet that "This is my preacher friend from the States." Jack is a perfect example of one who is more developed in one area than in another. He is a great example of not trying to shoehorn the development of disciples into a one-size-fits-all mold, but to build on an individual's natural strengths. With Jack it took several trips before he began to respond to anything 'spiritual' or 'religious.' Over the years he has come a long way. Now he even invites his friends to go to church with us.

The characteristics are actually quite similar to the corresponding phases of life development:

Life Stages	Discipleship Phases
Pre-stage • Not yet born	**Searching:** • Not yet 'born again' • Seeking meaning in life • Not connected to faith community
Infancy • Time of great discovery –know nothing about the world • Completely dependent upon someone more mature • Needs must be met – feeding, changing, holding, comforting	**Exploring** • Time of great discovery – know little about Christianity or life as a disciple - uncommitted • Completely dependent upon someone more mature • Needs must be met – relationships offered, discipleship explained, Scripture interpreted

the relevance of the message to their daily lives, and the witness to a commitment of this congregation to engage the community and make a difference.

Questions for Leaders and Coaches Related to Exploring Christ's Way:

- How are newcomers engaged by someone from the congregation?
- How are spiritual conversations encouraged for the development of understanding key Christian beliefs?
- What system is in place to help newcomers find a way to serve in a ministry?
- How are new believers introduced to the practice of reflecting on Scripture?
- What kind of opportunities are provided for the building of relationships?
- On a scale of 1–10, how applicable is the worship message to daily life?
- How does this congregation witness to its engagement of the surrounding community?
- How are members of the congregation encouraged to be engaged with those beyond the walls of the church?
- What support is offered by the church for inviting peers, friends, family, and neighbors to worship?
- How is the worship experience designed to invite people to take a next step in their faith journey?
- What is the practice of this congregation in following up with newcomers?
- What is the trend in "professions of faith" for this congregation?

The Beginning Phase

The **beginning** phase represents people who have made a commitment to be a disciple of Jesus. The question they are asking is "What?" or "What's it all about?" They are usually seeking help building the foundations of that relationship. This group is best served by providing introductory classes in the faith (e.g. the *Alpha* course) and foundational classes in discipleship practices (e.g. *Following Jesus, Foundations, Disciples Path*). Larger groups work well since this is primarily educational in focus. For smaller churches, having mentors from the congregation willing to work one-on-one with beginners in the journey seems to work well.

The **beginning** phase of discipleship is often accompanied by a sense of excitement as believers embark on a new journey in life. It is also a time when there is a great deal of uncertainty about how to live into this new calling. The church has an amazing opportunity to help provide a foundation for this new life in Christ.

Questions for Leaders and Coaches Related to Beginning a New Life in Christ:

- How does this congregation celebrate with people who have made a decision to follow Jesus?
- What kinds of connections are provided to help people discover what this new life will look like for them?
- How does the worship service equip people with tools for strengthening personal worship?
- What kind of training is provided for building the foundations of spiritual practices?
- How are people invited to be in some form of discipling relationship beyond the worship experience?
- What types of 'on-ramp' service/mission experiences are available to help people discover the joy of service?
- How does this congregation help people discover their gifts and passions for ministry?

The Growing Phase

The **growing** phase represents people who are moving into a more committed relationship with Jesus. They are asking the question "How?" or "How does it work?" They have moved into the 'disciple led' portion of the journey where the equipping of disciples becomes much more personal and individualized. Not everybody has the same needs. Some will want to explore more advanced spiritual practices, and others will long for a deeper understanding of how God is calling them to be in service to the community. In this stage we move from a one-size-fits-all to a more coach-like approach. Small groups tend to be the cornerstone of this phase of development, providing the opportunity for deeper exploration as we are exposed to stories and insights from a variety of fellow travelers. We have also found that discipleship coaching is a powerful tool in working with this group.

Those in the **growing** phase of discipleship have begun to realize that there is more to the journey than showing up for worship and having a daily devotional time. They begin to experience a longing for a deeper relationship with Jesus, a stronger sense of the presence of God in daily life, and a growing commitment to make a difference in the world.

Questions for Leaders and Coaches Related to Growing Our Walk in Christ:

- How is the congregation introduced to spiritual practices through worship experiences?
- What types of relationships are available to support people in their growth toward maturity?
- What classes are offered that invite participants to explore the spiritual disciplines?
- How does this congregation connect people with a variety of service/mission opportunities?
- How are people equipped to use their financial resources in ways that honor God?
- In what ways does the congregation encourage cross-cultural and cross-ethnic understanding and relationships?
- What opportunities are offered to the congregation to develop missional connections within other cultures?
- Is there a clear picture of what maturity as a disciple looks like for this congregation?

The Maturing Phase

The **maturing** phase represents people who are 'sold out to Jesus.' They have discovered that there is nothing more life-giving than being in the presence of Christ. These are disciples who have developed a strong spiritual life through experimenting with a variety of spiritual disciplines, and they are energetic in seeking new ways to deepen their experience of Jesus. They live with a focus on connecting with those who don't know Jesus at all, and they are excited about guiding the beginner disciples to discover more of Jesus. They have discovered that a life of discipleship is not about the accrual of personal blessings.

Questions for Leaders and Coaches Related to the Maturing Phase:

- What types of one-to-one relationships are available to support the continuing development of maturing disciples?
- How are disciples encouraged to build relationships outside of the church?
- What types of training and equipping are provided to develop maturing disciples for leadership in the congregation?
- How are maturing disciples connected to those beginning the discipling process to partner for their growth?

Several years ago, Willow Creek Community Church conducted the *Reveal* research project. While massive amounts of data were collected from the 1,000 churches in the project, some of the most helpful numbers captured what people said they needed from the church in order to progress from one phase of development to the next. This study produced some great insights, organizing them into five key themes.

But before we get into the specifics, let's explore a couple of things that may be surprising. As you review the graphic make some notes in the space below about what you observe: [2]

emc What people say they need from the church to support movement toward maturity:	Exploring	Beginning	Growing
Help developing a personal relationship with Jesus	68%	83%	87%
Compelling Worship Services	68%	75%	
A feeling of belonging	68%		
Help understanding the Bible	67%	82%	89%
Church leaders who model and constantly reinforce how to grow spiritually	66%	78%	84%
Challenge to grow and take next steps		74%	82%
Encouragement to take personal responsibility for spiritual growth			80%

Here are some things worth noticing:

A Feeling of Belonging: this response is found only in the movement from the exploring to the beginning phase of development. I think this is very interesting when viewed from the perspective of working with congregations who place a great emphasis on helping people feel like they belong. It is typical for congregations to do lots of 'fellowship-y' (my word) stuff to help people feel comfortable and connected. We do fellowship times, fellowship groups, fellowship dinners, and fellowship gatherings, and we even try to figure out how to get participants from different worship services together—often in a building or hall constructed solely for the purpose of gathering us in . . . fellowship! Apparently, however, when disciples are making the movement beyond the exploring phase, they already feel like they belong.

Compelling Worship Services: I want to be a little careful here. The research indicates that as disciples move from the beginning phase to the growing phase of development, the need for the church to provide compelling worship lessens. I do not think this is an indicator about the value of worship for these disciples. Nor is it an indicator related to the excellence with which worship is provided. I think it reflects a reality that disciples in the growing phase are no longer dependent upon the church-gathered-all-together to provide their only worship experiences. These disciples are creating their own personal worship spaces and building lifestyles of worship. Corporate worship is still important, but it is not the only source of worship experiences.

Notice also the increase in the percentages of persons indicating the need for support in:

- Understanding the Bible.
- Developing a personal relationship with Jesus.
- Church leaders who model and constantly reinforce how to grow spiritually.

At first glance this may seem counter-intuitive, but I think it reveals something many of us have experienced but have not known how to articulate. As we begin to grow in our experience of any new thing, our understanding is limited by the experiences we have had. But as our understanding deepens, we begin to see the greater possibilities and potential. For example, in the beginning of developing a personal relationship with Jesus, the focus may be on our commitment to living into a new understanding of life as a disciple. As we begin to encounter God in fresh ways, those experiences begin to open up new understandings of the presence of Christ and the power of the Holy Spirit at work. This in turn helps us to see the possibilities and the potential of the relationship.

Challenge to grow and take next steps: Note that this focus begins after the foundations are built in the beginning phase of development.

Encouragement to take personal responsibility for spiritual growth: This theme doesn't begin until we have been taught the foundational spiritual practices and are introduced to a variety of tools that are helpful in our continued development. The focus is on learning to feed ourselves and not to be dependent upon the church for our growth.

Help Understanding the Bible

Research by Willow Creek (as reported in the book *Move: What 1,000 Churches Reveal About Spiritual Growth*) identifies "help in understanding the Bible" as a need reported by the vast majority, no matter where they are in their journey toward maturity as a disciple of Jesus. In fact, as demonstrated on the table below, this desire to understand the Bible actually increases as we grow in our faith and discover the value of reflecting on the scriptures.

Seems pretty basic. You'd think we'd have this one covered!

We generally offer a full spectrum of biblical studies and discipleship classes, but this does not turn out to directly translate into people's perception that they really understand the Bible better. We provide an assortment of 'flavor of the month' studies by well-known preachers and video-based classes by popular, photogenic teachers which are great for highlighting particular themes (and also convenient and not too demanding, preparation-wise). But is that fully feeding people's deeper hunger? What we more rarely offer people is a pathway to learn the skills to study the Bible for themselves: how to use time-tested resources to discern truths on their own and how to apply such thoughtfully explored scriptural wisdom to their lives.

Have you noticed how the younger generation that has grown up with the convenience of GPS to get from point A to point B sometimes loses the ability to read a plain old map? Or having successfully followed the soothing and authoritative GPS guidance, they arrive safely at their practices. The first step to promote such leadership is to establish clear guidelines for those who will be selected to be leaders in a congregation. These guidelines should adhere to biblical principles, and to achieve maximum effect they should also be tailored to the particular personality of a given congregation. They should reflect the goal-defined expectations of all members of a congregation, but leaders are expected to be doing exactly that—leading the way.

For example, a person being considered for leadership must be:

- Regular in worship.
- Participating in an accountable discipleship relationship.
- Tithing.
- Serving in the community at least monthly.
- Building relationships with at least three people beyond the church to be Jesus in their lives and inviting at least three persons to church annually.

Notice that the last of these goals is specific in a way that establishes measurable accountability. These leadership guidelines will work best if given a specific metric by which each can be measured. 'Regular Attendance' can be defined any number of ways, but the point is for it to be defined, with all parties agreeing to the definition.

No goals are of value without accountability. That is another hallmark of real discipleship.

The complaints to this approach of recruiting leaders will be obvious: what if we can't find enough leaders who model and reinforce these spiritual practices who are also willing to serve? First, perhaps this process just means we have to recruit more deeply and thoughtfully, and secondly, perhaps it means we have too many leadership pigeonholes to fill to begin with.

The Challenge to Grow and Take Next Steps

This may come as a surprise for some, but the Willow Creek survey indicates that a large percentage of those beginning the journey and starting to grow as disciples really do sense that there is more to the process than what they have experienced so far. They've been doing the routine of a daily devotional guide and reading through the Bible in a year, but then they meet someone like you and realize that your connection with Jesus is so strong, it's like Jesus is speaking directly to you. They want that, too!

Those maturing disciples know what it takes to engage spiritual practices and grow in their relationship with Jesus. Those just starting the journey and those who are just beginning to discover the possibilities of the journey share the desire to be challenged to take the next steps and supported in actually taking those steps. If you think of the local church as a GPS device, our routine would too often be to describe the destination in elaborate, picturesque detail with stories and poetry that makes the listener just drool to want to be there—all of this accompanied by an inspirational soundtrack and state-of-the-art visuals. But when that inspired listener looks to us for turn-by-turn directions on how to get to this life-changing destination, she's stuck with more pictures of the destination (or maybe a voice that keeps repeating, "recalculating . . . recalculating").

One way to give emerging disciples the direction they need is to be clear at the end of a sermon or the conclusion of a worship experience exactly what it is you are hoping they will do in response. All too often the Scriptures have been exegeted well and great stories told, and then the service ends with "this has been the Word of God for the People of God, have a great week," and out the door with a hymn. We need to be clear about the invitation to take a step forward in discipleship. Describe for people what they are being invited to do to move their faith life forward.

Then, help them do it.

This ties directly into the need to have a well-developed path that believers can travel on the road of discipleship. If you know what that path is, then it is much easier to help people access it at the point that makes the most sense for them on their personal journey. One of the best ways to bring clarity to 'next step' conversations is to connect more recent disciples with more mature disciples by using:

- Accountable discipleship groups.
- Spiritual friends.
- Discipleship coaches.
- Spiritual Directors.

Different people prosper in different types of spiritual mentoring relationships. Having the widest possible points of intersection will result in the most comfortable (and fruitful) fit for any given individual. This is like moving from the impersonality of a GPS to the custom guidance of a personal tour guide (a guide who knows the territory well and can provide invaluable insights for getting the most out of the journey).

Encouragement to Take Personal Responsibility for Growth

As people move toward maturity, they should become less dependent on the local church to provide for their spiritual growth. They should begin to take responsibility for managing their own journey. They should begin to feed themselves! Isn't that what we all hope for with our own children? That they will develop the skills to feed and clothe themselves?

The strong tendency in the church seems to be around providing the fertile scriptural soil for growth, but often without the kind of trellis or frame that tender spiritual shoots need to give them a meaningful direction. We do semesters of classes with a wide variety of Bible Study offerings. We provide the best and newest of the DVD spiritual growth studies. But what people want and need from us is not just another big-name Bible Study or some news-relevant topic or self-help guide with some Bible verses thrown in for reference. What they really want is for us to teach them how to feed themselves.

emc³ What people say they need from the church to support movement toward maturity:	Exploring	Beginning	Growing
Help developing a personal relationship with Jesus	68%	83%	87%
Compelling Worship Services	68%	75%	
A feeling of belonging	68%		
Help understanding the Bible	67%	82%	89%
Church leaders who model and constantly reinforce how to grow spiritually	66%	78%	84%
Challenge to grow and take next steps		74%	82%
Encouragement to take personal responsibility for spiritual growth			80%

At this point it is obligatory to quote the infamous Chinese proverb: "Give a man a fish, feed him for a day. Teach a man to fish, feed him for a life-time." But think about our discipleship strategies from that perspective. What difference would it make if we taught these classes?

- **How to Study the Bible and Apply the Principles to Your Life** (rather than just absorbing a popular author's take on the Scripture, real tools for independently diving into the Word more deeply).

- **How to Listen to God through Prayer** (specific techniques for listening for God's voice rather than our filling all of the holy conversation with a recitation of our wants and woes).

- **Discerning God at Work in our Community and World** (interacting with our daily environment with a Spirit-powered radar for God's presence and possibilities).

- **Finding Guidance for Life through Prayerful Discernment** (using prayer and scripture as a path to practical wisdom).

- **Loving Others Like God Loves Them** (developing a deeper perspective to see each person living with their full potential as a child of God).

- **Discovering How God Has Wired You for Ministry** (understanding that everyone has a uniquely gifted role to play and being diligent about learning your own role).

- **Living a Lifestyle of Worship** (embracing a moment-to-moment communion with God rather than a once-a-week scripted encounter).

How game-changing would it be if we sent empowered disciples out to put these spiritual skills into action instead of expecting them to keep coming back for just another feeding time? These are the reimagined strategies that can produce leaders and grow disciples who (as a natural part of their mature discipleship) will begin producing other disciples. These are the confident and competent followers of Jesus who will change their communities and the world. What changes can you see such a shift in strategy producing in your own local faith community? What frustrations in disciple formation do you routinely encounter that might be addressed by such a shift?

The ultimate goal of all this is transformed lives. In contrast to the typical approach of Christian Education where people learn more about Jesus and are given hypothetical examples of what life might look like as a committed disciple, 'Discipleship' is focused on changing actual behaviors. Discipleship is not just about what we know. It is about what we do and ultimately who we are because of our relationship with Jesus.

The Real Discipleship Survey

The following matrix comes from a resource available through www.emc-3coaching.com, called the *Real Discipleship Survey.* It is a one-page summary of where disciples place themselves along a continuum of maturity in each of six dimensions of discipleship. In addition to the summary, a report is provided to the person who takes the survey describing the area of discipleship, identifying where the disciple placed themselves on the continuum (and what that means), and suggesting next steps to move toward maturity, along with providing suggested resources for help in getting there.

You will recognize these dimensions from earlier in this book. They are located in the left column of the matrix. Across the top of the matrix are four of the five phases of development presented previously. The *searching* phase is not included in this tool since it is designed to measure the level of transformation for those already involved in the ministry of the local church.

emc³	Exploring	Beginning	Growing	Maturing
A life of Worship	I attend worship when a friend invites me, when it is convenient, or when I feel a need.	I attend worship regularly, but I am growing to realize that I must attend to God every day.	I attend worship regularly and set aside time daily for personal worship.	I honor God in the ways I work, play, and engage others in relationships.
A life of Hospitality	I am curiously drawn to the Christians who graciously accept me as if I belong with them already.	I am called not only to receive, but also to offer God's gracious acceptance to others.	I seek to relate to others both in the church and beyond in ways that reflect God's hospitality to me.	I intentionally seek to build relationships with unchurched people in order to share God's love.
A life open to Jesus	I am drawn to the story of God's love and am beginning to explore the scriptures for myself.	I am developing a daily practice of prayer, scripture, and devotional reading, opening myself to God.	I am exploring new spiritual disciplines and experience a greater level of intimacy with God.	I am taking responsibility for my own growth through the daily practice of spiritual disciplines.
I life of obeying Jesus	I understand more about Jesus' teaching through Bible Study classes and my own reading.	I have accepted the call to be a follower of Jesus Christ and am committed to being part of the church, becoming like Jesus and serving others.	I am daily seeking to apply the teaching of scripture to my own life.	I am partnering with God to help others grow in openness and obedience to Christ.
A life of Service	I am often amazed at the way some disciples selflessly serve others and I want to make a difference as well.	I know Christ invites me to join him serving others and I'm discovering how God has gifted me to do this.	I experiment with serving in different areas as I discover my gifts, talents, and passions.	I join Jesus in mission to others using my God-given gifts, talents and passions.
A life of Generosity	I give some when I attend worship.	I am giving more and more regularly	I am tithing and reconsidering how I spend the other 90%.	I am tithing and consciously reordering my life to free up more resources to honor God and bless others.

© Maynard, 2014

For each of the dimensions of discipleship—with the exception of "A Life Opening to Jesus"—as the disciple moves from the left side of the matrix to the right side, there is a shift in focus from being about ourselves to being about others. For example, in "A Life of Hospitality," the exploring phase is all about how accepted the disciple feels and how they experience a sense of belonging. In the maturing phase though, the focus shifts from being about ourselves to being about others—specifically those outside of the church. This is the shift described as we move from adolescence to adulthood. The exception to this framework is "A Life Opening to Jesus." Maturity in this dimension is still focused on the disciple, but in a way that reflects that the disciple is taking responsibility for his or her own spiritual journey rather than being dependent upon the church to meet all of their needs.

For the vast majority of us, we will find that we are at different levels of maturity in the various dimensions of discipleship. For example, some people are very mature when it comes to offering themselves to "A Life of Service," but find themselves at a beginning phase in "A Life Obeying Jesus." This is perfectly natural. All of us have certain areas of strength and other areas that are more of an opportunity for development.

The value of the *Real Discipleship Survey* is that it points us to our current reality in our life as a disciple. It is not a 'cast in concrete' or 'fit in my box' kind of resource. It is a tool to help us consider where we are in our journey toward maturity and where it is that we want to go. The best use for this resource is that of starting a conversation about your journey.

You may have noticed that the columns titled "Growing" and "Maturing" are shaded in darker grays in the background. This is my way of indicating that people with that level of discipleship are moving toward the place where they could be considered for leadership within a congregation. I operate from the perspective that those being considered for leadership within a congregation must be the most mature in their discipleship journey that the church has to offer. Where the leaders go, so goes the church. If you want your church to be generous, the leaders must exhibit a life of generosity. If you want your church to be reaching people who don't yet know the love of Jesus, your leaders must be mature in their life of hospitality. If you want to make a difference in your community, your leaders must be mature in a life of service. Where the leaders go, so goes the church. This tool is a good resource of helping select maturing disciples for leadership in the local church.

The *Real Discipleship Survey* is also a great tool for helping the discipleship ministries team in a local congregation identify the areas in the discipleship process that need more support to develop maturing disciples. When a church completes the survey, the administrator receives a report in the form of a matrix that indicates the percentage of people who placed themselves in each of the levels of maturity for each dimension of discipleship.

The following graphic is provided as an example. It is the composite result from a local congregation:

	Exploring	Beginning	Growing	Maturing
A Life of Worship	0%	26%	47%	26%
A Life of Hospitality	1%	29%	56%	1%
A Life Open to Jesus	15%	21%	38%	26%
A Life Obeying Jesus	1%	56%	29%	1%
A Life of Service	18%	32%	18%	32%
A Life of Generosity	1%	23%	20%	44%

With only a quick glance you will notice that there are two areas in the "Maturing" column that have only a 1% response from participants. This means that only 1% of the participants in this representative sampling indicated that they were, for example, building intentional relationships with people beyond the church in order to introduce them to God's love for them. This congregation is strong in the phases of being welcoming and nice to others, but there is little focus on faith-sharing or personal evangelism. This is an area that will need to be strengthened if this church is to fulfill its mission of making disciples of Jesus Christ.

Similarly, only 1% of the participants indicated that they were in partnership with someone in the beginning phases of the discipleship process to help them grow toward maturity. Again, this is an area of opportunity as we set expectations for discipleship and equip people to mentor, coach, and lead small groups. We must remind ourselves constantly, as we make decisions and allocate resources, that the goal of an intentional process for discipleship is to support the development of maturing disciples of Jesus Christ who live life differently—who exhibit behaviors that reflect that growing relationship. Consider the following:

Would our churches be more vital? More effective? More transforming? If people . . .

- Lived lives honoring God in the ways they worked, played, and engaged others?

- Intentionally built relationships in order to be Christ to someone?

- Took responsibility for their own spiritual growth?

- Discipled someone else, helping them move toward maturity?

- Used their gifts and talents to serve others?

- Lived within margins in order to bless others?

Questions for Reflection

1. What process is in place within your congregation to:

   • Equip members/participants to build relationships with those outside the church (friends, neighbors, acquaintances, community)?

   • Engage uncommitted persons exploring the faith to answer questions and discover the possibilities for life as a disciple of Jesus Christ?

   • Train new believers in the basic theological understandings and spiritual practices that will serve as a foundation for the journey as a disciple?

   • Provide growing disciples the tools, relationships, practices that will serve as catalysts for engaging the life as a disciple more fully?

   • Build capacity as leaders for the congregation in growing maturing disciples, supporting the ministries of the church, and engaging the community?

2. How does your church teach disciples to "feed themselves"?

3. What expectations are set for those serving in leadership within the congregation?

chapter three

Discipleship As A "Contact Sport"

Relationship connections
as the pathway to discipleship

"He who walks with the wise grows wise." – Proverbs 13:20

"People come to churches expecting to grow; it is up to church leaders to provide opportunities for growth." –Albert Winesman

An Intentional Discipleship Process

There's a great clip on YouTube titled "50th Anniversary—Rock Climbing Wall." It is worth your time to take a few minutes and watch this home-made video documenting a group of friends on a cruise ship who decided to try out the rock climbing wall.

As you watch, make notes below about what you see and hear:

The chances are good that you identified some of the following:

- Lots of encouragement ("good job").
- The right equipment.
- Instruction ("move your foot up just a little to the right").
- A safety line (nobody can get hurt).
- Acceptance of whatever level of success people choose to reach.
- Different pathways to success.
- People who fulfill different roles depending on where their fellow participants are in the process.
- Lots of fun!

While a little unusual, I think this rock climbing experience is a great metaphor for an intentional discipleship process. All the things that were identified as supporting the rock-climbing adventure as experienced by these folks in the video, need to be a part of the discipleship process experienced by the people in our churches. However, for many of us who grew up as part of a local congregation, this is not the discipleship process that we actually experienced. The models for how to become like Jesus have traditionally been more restrictive, less interactive, and not usually described as lots of fun.

Discipleship Models from Current Church Culture

In current church culture, there seem to be three primary approaches. The first is the Discipleship Model. The most popular of these is the 'Baseball Diamond' model, developed by Rick Warren and Saddleback Church: [1]

Here's the description straight from Saddleback's web site:

> Our Christian Life And Service Seminars (C.L.A.S.S.) teach you all about what it looks like to follow Christ and gives you the tools you need for each step of the journey. Start with Class 101 and see how God transforms your life as you grow in your faith.
>
> Class 101 is a great step for learning about the history of Saddleback Church, what we believe, and how to become a member of the Saddleback family. You'll also have the opportunity to get baptized after class. In Class 201 you can find out what it means to be more like Jesus, learn how to spend time with God through prayer and Bible study, discover the importance of tithing, and understand the value of community. In Class 301 you will learn how God can use your Spiritual gifts, Heart (passions), Abilities, Personality, and Experiences to help to others. Class 401 will help you discover your calling, learn how to share your story with others, write down your personal testimony, and see how to impact the world around you with Christ's love. ²

A second approach is the Christian Education Model. The general philosophy undergirding this approach is that if people are simply exposed to a variety of 'courses' providing instruction about the scriptures or spiritual practices or current issues, they will change the ways in which they think and act and become more like Jesus. This common approach is often described in academic terms and schedules: [3]

Register online by visiting the small groups section of www.[...] or in person on Sundays between August 23, 2009 and September 6, 2009

Class/Small Group	Day	Start Date	Time	Facilitator	Location	Length	Childcare	Book Fee*	Nextstep
I Want to Believe...But I have Questions!	Monday	07-Sept	7:00PM	Pastor Dave	PRF	18 weeks	TBD	none	SHOW
For Heaven's Sake	Saturday	03-Oct	3:00PM	Diane Hendricks	PRF	One Day	TBD	none	SHOW
The Disciple's Cross	Wednesday	09-Sept	7:00pm	Twila Beyer	PRF	6 weeks	yes - fee	$15	KNOW
Developing a Devotional Life	Monday	31-Aug	7:00 PM	Jeff Strecker	PRF	11 weeks	TBD	$11	KNOW
Esther: It's Hard to be a Woman	Wednesday	09-Sept	9:00AM	Kendra Ochiuzzo	PRF	10 weeks	yes - fee	$16	KNOW
Prayer Study	Tuesday	08-Sept	7:00PM	Diane Eagle	PRF	10 Weeks	TBD	TBD	KNOW
Young Adult Bible Study	TBD	TBD	7:00 PM	Tim Wadle	PRF	TBD	TBD	TBD	KNOW
Good Sense	Thursday	17-Sept	6:30PM	Dave Llewellyn	PRF	7 weeks	TBD	TBD	GROW
Men of Honor	Wednesday	09-Sept	7:00PM	Jerry Johnson	PRF	Ongoing	yes - fee	none	GROW
And Then I had Teenagers	Wednesday	09-Sept	7:00 PM	Debbie Moenning	PRF	12 weeks	yes - fee	$12	GROW
Homebuilders Marriage Study	Tuesday	08-Sept	7:00PM	Jon & Bonnie Fernandez	PRF	TBD	TBD	$15	GROW
The Truth Project	Wednesday	09-Sept	7:00PM	Phillip Stephens	TBD	13 weeks	yes - fee	TBD	GROW
Couple's Bible Study	Friday	18-Sept	7:00PM	Rob & Alicia Gordon	Gordon Home	TBD	TBD	TBD	GROW
Creative Correction	Wednesday	09-Sept	7:00PM	Diane Hendricks	PRF	7 weeks	yes-fee	$16	GROW
When Women Walk Alone	Thursday	10-Sept	7:00 PM	Sandy Koref	PRF	10 weeks	TBD	$15	GROW
The Disciple's Personality/Victory	Tuesdays	15-Sept	7:00PM	Tim King	PRF	12 Weeks	TBD	$15	GROW
The Disciple's Mission	TBD	TBD	TBD	TBD	PRF	6 weeks	TBD	TBD	GO
Just Walk Across The Room	TBD	TBD	TBD	TBD	PRF	TBD	TBD	TBD	GO

* Full or partial scholarships are available for materials fees. Please contact the facilitator for information.

There is nothing wrong with a strong Christian Education program in a local congregation. It's just not the same thing as discipleship. As we've observed before, discipleship is not just about information, it is about transformation.

A third approach to discipleship is the laissez-faire attitude which is found in more congregations than we would like to admit. This approach meets the definition of "letting things take their own course, without interfering." [4] There are no expectations set, no direction given, no conversations initiated, and no commitments made. It's as if the church thinks that if people simply come to worship enough they will become growing maturing disciples by osmosis.

I think we need to be much more intentional.

The Importance of Relationships

It all starts with relationships. Discipleship is a contact sport. Discipleship happens in relationships. Usually it includes several different kinds of relationships as we move toward maturity. We will explore several different types of relationships and how to draw on those relationships as an effective resource to fuel the discipleship journey. We'll consider these relationships in an order based on the phases of development laid out in detail in earlier chapters. Some of the applications overlap.

Relational Evangelism: As previously noted, most people who come to church (60-80%) are introduced to Jesus through a one-to-one relationship. I call this *Incarnational Hospitality* as discussed back in the opening chapter on clarity. Of course, other types of relationships come into play at this point in the journey as well (the *searching* phase): servant evangelism, meet-up groups, classes, etc.

Hierarchical Models for Discipleship

Faith Guides/Mentors/Hospitality Angels

When people show up at church for the first time, checking things out (the *exploring* phase), the most important thing that can happen is for someone to be intentional about building a relationship with them. It is this connection that in most cases will determine whether the person/family will return.

For those who are brand new to the idea of discipleship, a more specialized type of relational connection may be helpful. Many churches are developing an intentional ministry team that bridges the gap between hospitality and discipleship. These team members are sometimes called Faith Guides or Mentors. Their role is to offer a longer-term relationship (sometimes over several weeks or months) to the explorer, thus giving them the opportunity to ask questions and talk about what they are experiencing as they become engaged with a community of faith. Some of the questions that may come up:

- Why should I become a disciple?
- Who is Jesus?
- What do I have to do to live as a disciple?
- What do I have to give up?
- What do I get out of being a disciple?
- Can I still keep my non-Christian friends?
- What about people who call themselves Christians but don't live like it?

For those who are already committed disciples entering into a new community of faith, these Faith Guides or Mentors have conversations with the newcomers and help them figure out how to get connected in a meaningful and supportive way, perhaps in making a connection with a small group leader or a ministry/service team where the newcomer has a passion for serving. This is, of course, a much more inviting and supportive way to help people become assimilated than giving them a brochure listing opportunities for spiritual development and service.

For those who are brand new to the idea of Christianity and are not sure they are ready to explore a full-on commitment to discipleship, it is important that they feel like they can 'fit in' with this community of faith. Some churches are experimenting with Hospitality Angels (or some other equally adorable and unthreatening name) who reach out to new faces in worship, introduce guests to staff and pastor, and sometimes even take them to lunch following worship to get to know them better and lay the groundwork for a stronger relationship.

Paul-Timothy Relationships (The Single Parent Model)

As captured by the name, this model is built on the relationship described in the New Testament between Paul and his protégé, Timothy. The Apostle Paul served as a mentor and guide to the young and inexperienced Timothy, who steadily grew in stature and maturity, eventually becoming a co-worker and fellow traveler with Paul and well-respected leader in his own right.

This approach to discipleship is often encouraged as a bridge from evangelism to discipleship, which is a natural flow or process. It draws on the strong bonding component of 'relational evangelism' and provides a natural movement to a 'training' phase for discipleship. There are even materials that are available for focusing conversations around the important stuff of discipleship (e.g. *Discipleship Essentials,* by Greg Ogden*).*

The Paul-Timothy Model for discipleship has been a cornerstone of discipling relationships for several decades. It is the model most notably used by the groups like the Navigators, who use the terminology of life-to-life discipleship. There is often an unspoken assumption that this approach to discipleship is the biblically mandated universal paradigm, such as in the following description from Paul Stanley and J. Robert Clinton:

> Discipling is a process in which a more experienced follower of Christ shares with a newer believer the commitment, understanding and basic skills necessary to know and obey Jesus Christ as Lord. [5]

Ogden identifies some key assumptions which drive this model for discipleship:

- Older person with a younger person (like a father-son relationship).
- More spiritually mature with less spiritually mature.
- Teacher-student relationship (learned with the unlearned).
- More experienced with the less experienced.
- One in authority over one under authority.

Ogden also identifies some of the dynamics of this type of relationship:

- The 'more mature' disciple carries the responsibility.
- There is a hierarchy that may result in dependency.
- The hierarchical nature may limit interchange or dialogue.
- This relationship often does not reproduce. [6]

The reproduction issue is a pretty big deal since this approach is often touted as the way to answer the call of the Great Commission to disciple the whole world. There are arguably, however, a couple of inherent problems with this approach. First, it is often the case that maturing disciples don't feel ready or equipped to disciple someone else. Second, due to the relationship flowing from the more mature to the less mature disciple, the person being discipled also feels ill-equipped to disciple someone else. In his research, Ogden discovered that many of these issues can be successfully addressed by adding a third person into the discipling mix.

Triads (A Very Small Group Model)

This model of discipleship again might form a bridge from the hospitality-focused, relational evangelism to beginning level discipleship, or if we use the terminology employed earlier in this book, we would say this model supports the movement from *exploring* to *beginning*.

Essentially a very small group, triads are three people connecting in a discipling relationship. There is still a more mature disciple, but the additional person changes the dynamics from hierarchical to relational and from a back-and-forth dialogue to a dynamic interchange. In other words, it moves from a top-down "let me tell you how to do this" dynamic to a conversation between friends trying to live into who Jesus is calling them to be. A couple of added benefits to this approach include the wisdom found in numbers and a greater willingness for participants to then form similar groups to disciple others. [7]

Egalitarian Small Group Models

First, a Word on Christian Education Classes

I make a fairly strong distinction between Christian Education and discipleship. The former, of course, focuses on learning about Jesus, and the latter focuses on becoming more like Jesus. This distinction carries over into the realm of Christian Education Classes and Small Group ministries. I think they are two different things, at least in the way that most of them are executed. The former is information-driven, while the latter is transformation-driven.

In the typical classroom academic model, there is a teacher and students (or facilitator and group) who may hold an opening prayer and closing prayer within the class structure, but the focus is on sharing information and gaining insights into the Scripture/church/Christian life. It is the exceptional Christian Education class that actually explores with participants what it might look like to apply that information to the daily business of living. Even further out is the class that asks for personal commitments and holds people accountable. Having said this, I also want to acknowledge the great value of Christian Education and the teaching role within the

Church. I am a former educator (at the university level). My top-ranking spiritual gift has always been teaching. I always taught Bible study classes and prayer classes as part of my ministry in the local church.

But having established my credentials as a passionate educator, I have come to understand that there is an extraordinary opportunity that many of our churches are missing during the beginning phase of the discipleship journey. For those who have decided to follow Christ, but are just taking the first steps, the big question is "What do I need to do?" In all honesty, we miss a logical place to answer this critical question. We encourage people to be hungry for a strong educational foundation in basic spiritual practices and basic Christian beliefs, but we often don't provide it. It's like that frustrating moment when you drive up to the KFC drive-through and place your order, only to be asked if you can pull forward to wait because they are out of chicken!

For some reason, we seem to think people will get this stuff by osmosis—just sitting in the pews! But there are people who have been sitting in our pews for a very long time who still don't know how to pray, or reflect on Scripture, or live in authentic relationships, or share their faith, or use their resources wisely, or figure out how to serve others. And don't get me started on theological understandings. We'll come back to this in the next section, but for now let's recognize the huge gap at the beginning of the process of discipleship, and let's recognize that Christian Education can play a significant role in supporting the work of making disciples.

Connect Groups

It's a really big jump for those beginning the discipling process, especially those in the *exploring* phase of development, to commit to an intentional discipleship group with a strong teaching component and accountability. One of the models to bridge the gap between connecting people relationally (hospitality as a starting point in discipleship) and connecting people in an intentional discipleship focus is the Connect Group.

These groups are based on affinity, and the connecting points are almost limitless. For example:

- Spiritual support/community.
- Food.
- Prayer.
- Service projects.
- Bible study.

- Fun and fellowship.
- Exercise/stress management.
- Neighborhoods.
- Hobbies and mutual interests.
- Age level activities.
- Sports activities (biking, hiking, softball, bowling, etc.).
- Neighborhood game nights.
- Support groups.

In my first appointment as a pastor, my wife, Becky, hosted a Mexican cooking class at our home. She didn't teach the class—not her area of expertise. But the class took place in our kitchen. There were, of course, a couple of women from the church and several others from the neighborhood and some other friends who had been invited. It was a great several weeks for me as I got to eat freshly made Mexican dishes.

The food was terrific, but even better was the connection formed by the women in this group. I know this will surprise you, but they didn't just talk about how to create wonderful meals. They talked about their families and their jobs and their struggles and joys and even their faith. You get the idea. Statistics are clear that for people to stay active in any congregation, they need at least six relationships with people to be formed during the first six months. If this doesn't happen, they often drift away. What better way to help people build relationships than to get them together with a group of people who like to do the same things they like to do?

As I work with congregations using this model/approach to get people connected to each other, I also encourage them to recognize it as the wonderful opportunity it is to help people begin to get connected to Jesus. No hard sell stuff here! I ask Connect Groups affiliated with a congregation to do three simple things when they gather:

- Pray together for the needs of the group (connecting to the body of Christ).
- Share a brief devotion or Scripture selection (becoming more like Jesus).
- Do something as a group every few weeks that makes a difference in the community beyond the church (joining Jesus in ministry).

These will be addressed more fully as we take a closer look at the 3-B model. But for now I hope you will see that a commitment to implementing just these three basic connecting points can help people begin to think of themselves within the framework of discipleship.

The 3-B Model for Small Groups

For disciples moving from the beginning phase of the journey to the growing phase, a couple of factors come into play. First, there is a strong sense that there is something more to this life as a disciple than what they have experienced up to this point. They begin their morning with the Upper Room online daily devotional (or another of the hundreds of possible resources). They dutifully read their provided Bible verse, meditate upon a brief reflection, and earnestly pray the suggested one-sentence prayer. This has become part of their daily routine. But then they meet someone like you who seems to have a direct line to God! They want that, too. So the question becomes, how? How do I get from here to there?

For disciples at this stage of their journey, one of the tried-and-true ways for picking up the spiritual skill set that leads to greater growth is to be in a continuous conversation with other like-minded pilgrims. This is the function of the classic small group. I have used a pattern I call the 3-B Model for small groups. It is built around the definition of discipleship presented previously:

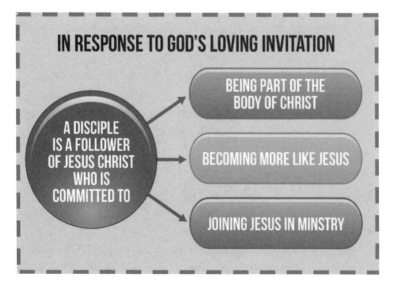

Small groups are asked to frame their time together around the 3 B's of:

- **B**elong = Being part of the body of Christ—a focus on building relationships with each other and with God (worship).
- **B**ecome = Becoming more like Jesus—a focus on studying and applying Scripture to our lives (identifying next steps) and being accountable to the group for our progress.
- **B**e = Being Christ to the world—a focus on joining Jesus in ministry/mission to the world.

In my 'tribe' (the denomination of which I have been a part of ministry leadership), there are several statistical measures that are tracked as indicators of church health. One of them is described as "the number of persons in discipleship groups." While this is often touted as a way to measure the level of discipleship happening in a congregation, I don't think it is really accurate as a true measure of transformation. What it really measures is the number of people we can convince to join a small group.

A step forward in the use of this statistical measure would be to more clearly define what a small group does. Otherwise, how do you determine if a particular group is accomplishing your goals for transformation? Is the choir a small group? What about the praise team? Or the UMW? Or the mission team? Or a Bible study? In my congregation, we described small groups as those following the 3-B framework. If you wanted to be considered a small group that was living up to our expectations for how we would promote and nurture transformation, you had to do three things:

- Have a time of fellowship (relationship building) and worship.
- Have some type of focus on becoming more like Jesus—studying Scripture, developing spiritual practices.
- Do some kind of service beyond the walls of the church every month or two.

Any group could become an official Discipling Small Group by using the three guidelines as a framing tool for their time together.

Wesley Fellowship Groups

Retired Bishop Dick Wills, in his last appointment to a local church (Christ United Methodist Church in Ft. Lauderdale), developed a small group ministry that became a model for many congregations across the country, called Wesley Fellowship Groups. These groups, comprised of four to five persons, met regularly following a 'recipe' of five ingredients:

- **Fellowship**: Meets the need to belong. People get to know and love one another. Be sure to play! Fun is essential to group health.
- **Worship**: Gives the opportunity to connect with God. Listen to/ sing praises. Share personal prayer concerns and offer prayer for those in need. Encourage participants to keep a journal.
- **Study**: In study we discover the truths of the Bible and discuss how to apply those to our lives. Some groups use a coaching approach to identifying next steps, gaining commitment for transformational change.
- **Accountability**: This is 'self-disclosure' to the group. It is when we ask the group to help us honor our most sacred commitments (e.g. prayer habits, family commitments, service, etc.).
- **Mission**: The journey inward must lead to the journey outward. The group engages in a ministry together at least once a quarter (once a month is recommended). We need to give as well as receive!

Like the 3-B model, this is a great format for those committed to growing as disciples of Jesus Christ.

Covenant Discipleship Groups

Covenant relationships and accountability are also at the heart of the Methodist Movement begun by John Wesley (because they are at the heart of any transformational process of discipleship). In Wesley's model, community and authentic relationships were supported through Class Meetings that featured a high level of accountability using a Covenant of Discipleship. Consider the following common elements of such a Covenant.

A Covenant of Discipleship

____ I will pray each day, privately, with my family and friends, and for my covenant members.

____ I will read and study the Scriptures each day according to a plan.

____ I will worship each Sunday unless prevented and receive the Sacrament of Communion when available.

____ I will heed the warnings of the Holy Spirit not to sin against God or my neighbor.

___ I will heed the promptings of the Holy Spirit to serve God and my neighbor.

___ I will prayerfully seek to care for my family and home and seek to help someone in need each day.

___ I will prayerfully care for my body and for the world in which I live.

___ I will prayerfully plan the stewardship of my resources.

___ I will share in Christian fellowship each week where I will be accountable for my discipleship.

This level of accountability in a small group model is usually most effective for those disciples moving from the growing phase to the maturing phase. Notice that there is less focus on living into the 'how' of discipleship and a greater focus on being more like Jesus. While other types of small groups had a strong element of 'teaching' or 'learning,' this covenant is intended to form a way of being in relationship with God and others.

The Covenant Discipleship Group is modeled in the tradition of the early Methodist Class Meetings. These groups would usually meet weekly and have from five to eight participants. Each group had a leader who facilitated discussion tied to accountability to the covenant and who also occasionally did some teaching around a theme or issue that arose during the conversation. The class leader would ask questions related to the covenant, then amplify by asking another question, offering encouragement, and sometimes giving advice. This type of group did not generally follow a defined curriculum, as noted by Kevin Watson in *The Class Meeting: Reclaiming a Forgotten (And Essential) Small Group Experience*:

> Rather than transferring information or ideas about Christianity, the early Methodist Class Meeting was focused on helping people come to know Jesus Christ and learn how to give every part of their lives to loving and serving Christ. [8]

In several tribes, the strongest reflection of accountable discipleship comes from the spiritual formation experience called in its various forms the Emmaus Walk or De Colores (or Cursillo or Via de Christo). The most transformative part of the experience is NOT the retreat weekend itself (although it is a powerful experience). It is the small accountability groups in which participants are encouraged to participate following the weekend experience. This is where transformed lives occur.

Discipling Partnerships

In a Procrustean world where a "one size fits all" small group is the answer to every question about how to create an intentional process for discipleship, we are discovering that the models we assumed we had perfected don't always work the way we thought they did—in fact, some of them are broken. But it doesn't have to be "it is what it is." Those outside the church are experiencing a dramatic cultural shift in the thinking of colleges, the workplace, and even in High School settings, as there is a concerted move toward customization, personalization, and do-it-yourself strategies.

Reggie McNeal, in *Missional Renaissance,* calls us to make this same kind of shift in the Church, moving from Program Development to People Development:

> The program-driven church came of age as the ultimate expression of the modern world's ability to achieve mass standardization . . . [which] when applied to the church world . . . meant . . . the development of widespread uniformity of   expectations . . . [and] standardized approaches treated people as market segments by age, gender, and life circumstance (college student, single or married, and so on. . . .) This process took on a life of its own. It wasn't long before the need to maintain these programs reversed the relationship between people and programs. People, once considered beneficiaries of program delivery, now become resources (possessors of time, talent, and money) to feed the program. . . .

> People are no longer going to let the church or church leaders provide the template for their spiritual journeys. Postmoderns do not know why they should have to search for God on church time and church real estate. Nor do people automatically believe that other people know what's best for them or that one organization can meet all their needs. . . .

> However . . . people will accept help in shaping their spiritual path. In fact, they welcome it, especially from people they respect and trust, who seem to have their best interests at heart. [9]

The following are some discipling partnerships that exemplify the type of help people will embrace.

Mentors

For those disciples in the growing phase or maturing phase of development, there is often a desire to become proficient in a particular spiritual practice or even to identify a particular person and want to become like them in the spiritual journey. A mentoring relationship is a great tool for someone in this growth mode.

In a mentoring relationship, there are generally two persons:

- One who is very good at a particular spiritual practice or who leads a life of discipleship that is particularly attractive to others.
- One who wants to develop a particular spiritual practice or who seeks to emulate the lifestyle of a particular maturing disciple.

In a mentoring relationship, the more skilled (advanced, developed, mature) disciple commits to helping a less skilled (less advanced, less developed, less mature) disciple develop their level of competency in a particular area (often referred to as 'pouring into').

In my first appointment as a pastor, I became friends with a church member by the name of Margrit. She was in her mid-eighties at the time, but still a disciple on fire. When she prayed, it was like she had a direct line to God. During a spiritual formation retreat I was facilitating at our Conference Life Enrichment Center, Margrit was a participant. I was getting my stuff to my room, but the key to the room wouldn't work. I was very frustrated. My wife, Becky, tried the key as well, but she couldn't get it to work either. I took the key back to the front desk and asked for a key that would actually open the room. I was, of course, given a replacement with sincere apologies. But that key wouldn't open the room either. Then Margrit came walking by and asked what was wrong. We explained the situation and Margrit asked if she could see the key. Then she did the weirdest thing I had ever seen. Margrit sat down on a porch swing and began to pray over the key. You guessed it! When she handed the key back, it opened the door on the first try.

When I grow up I want to be like Margrit.

That's what the beginning of a mentoring relationship looks like. The desire to be like—or develop a set of skills like—someone you have recognized as a more mature disciple. Our tendency in the church is to send people to classes to learn how to do things. I think we are missing a great opportunity, because a mentoring relationship is bigger than just learning how to do something. Through a mentoring relationship, we also begin to develop the same heart as the mentor. And that's how lives become transformed. The following graphic represents some of the types of mentoring relationships that are possible:

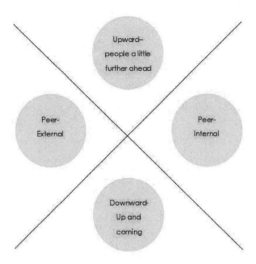

The "Upward" label represents the traditional type of relationship presented previously where you are seeking to be mentored by someone else.

The "Downward" label represents the possibility of you mentoring someone else. It is important to remember that you don't have to be an expert . . . just a couple of steps ahead.

The "Peer–External" label represents a relationship with someone from outside the organization who has a skill you want to develop, and the "Peer–Internal" label represents the same scenario, but with the desirable skill belonging to someone from within the organization.

Tom Bandy, in his book, *Christian Mentoring,* suggests that "spiritual growth tends to be marked by seven breakthrough experiences":

- Connect the seeker with his or her own intimate experience of Christ.

- Guide the seeker to develop spiritual habits for daily living.

- Guide the seeker to explore his or her authenticity as a human being.

- Challenge the seeker to confront manipulation and temptation.

- Connect the seeker with the accountability of a faith community.

- Encourage the seeker to discern his or her own personal mission in life.

- Release the seeker to God's Mercy. [10]

Discipleship Coaching

Coaching is a partnership through which the coach helps the coachee, in this case the disciple, figure out what they want to accomplish, set a goal, develop a plan, consider the obstacles, and then provide accountability as the coachee works the plan.

Steve Ogne and Tim Roehl, in their book, *Transformissional Coaching,* use the letters of the word coach to construct an acronym that defines the coaching process:

> **C** = Come alongside.
>
> **O** = Observe.
>
> **A** = Ask powerful questions.
>
> **C** = Consider options.
>
> **H** = Hold accountable.

I think discipleship coaching may be the most contemporary expression of the Wesleyan movement of accountable discipleship. The whole focus is on the disciple and what they want to accomplish (there is no prescribed curriculum). The role of the coach is to help them get there. Consider the following from Chad Hall, Bill Copper, and Kathryn McElveen in *Faith Coaching* (their term for discipleship coaching):

> Coaching appeals to people because it is a highly relational and personalized approach for having the kind of conversations that move a person toward his potential. A coach walks alongside the person being coached, helping him determine where the focus of the conversation needs to be, exploring new possibilities related to that topic, and determining what meaningful actions should be taken. The coach is also there for just-in-time accountability and to act as a sounding board.

> Coaching is certainly a customized learning and developmental approach, one that makes didactic and procedural approaches look like off-the-rack suits compared to the beautifully hand-tailored ones, customized to fit a unique body. Sure, the off-the-rack suit will cover you, but the tailored suit fits you so well you actually take pleasure in wearing it. People who are committed to development tend to prefer coaching over classroom or training approaches   because coaching is able to address the precise needs of individuals much more effectively. [11]

So, for example, the person being coached (the disciple) has realized that their spiritual practices have become routine and they want to try something different than the standard daily devotional. They yearn for a deeper sense of God's presence. The discipleship coach might then focus on the following elements of the conversation:

- Determine what the disciple has been doing.
- Ask questions about what an ideal time with God might look like.
- Explore some options for accomplishing that goal (e.g. other spiritual practices, different style of time with God).
- Build a plan for trying something new.
- Ask about how the plan worked (next conversation).

In the entire conversation the disciple sets the agenda, decides what to work on, determines what the next steps might be, and commits to a plan. Even the accountability factor is focused on the disciple—they are accountable to themselves. The discipleship coach just helps them organize their thoughts, gives them some guidance, and checks in with them. The following graphic demonstrates the flow of a typical coaching conversation:

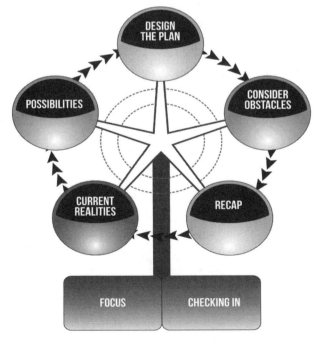

I believe that discipleship coaching is one of the most effective tools for helping disciples grow toward maturity. EMC3 Coaching provides training in discipleship coaching designed to equip coaches to provide this ministry for local congregations. This six hour training introduces participants to basic coaching skills and the coaching conversation model. Using the *Real Discipleship Survey*, disciples discover their current reality and determine goals for continued growth. A *Train-the-Trainer* workshop is also available to equip trainers in Conferences and Districts to provide *Discipleship Coaching Training* for local churches in their area.

Spiritual Direction

Spiritual Direction is a specialized partnership (in some ways similar to Discipleship Coaching) where a Spiritual Director partners with a disciple over a long-term relationship to help them pay attention to how God is at work in their lives. A Spiritual Director usually has between one and two years of formal training to serve in this role. Once they begin working with individual disciples, there is no curriculum to be followed, no formal pattern for the conversations that unfold, and no set expectation for action steps. Consider the following excerpt from Margaret Guenther in *Holy Listening: The Art of Spiritual Direction*:

> Spiritual direction, as a work of love, is also a work of freedom. The director is willing to let be, to love with an open hand. Hers is a contemplative love, immune from temptation to devour, possess, or manipulate. . . . [T]he director . . . has faith in the process of growth and change—and even more faith in the power of God's grace. This is a ministry of hope and newness that enlivens, and even helps define. . . . Spiritual direction is about entertaining these troublesome angels who turn up at surprising and rarely convenient times and places . . . about recognizing those angels and helping our sisters and brothers who entrust themselves to us to be joyously attentive. . . . [12]

Let's pull all the pieces together using the graphic below to help identify what kind of relationships might be most helpful in the different phases of development:

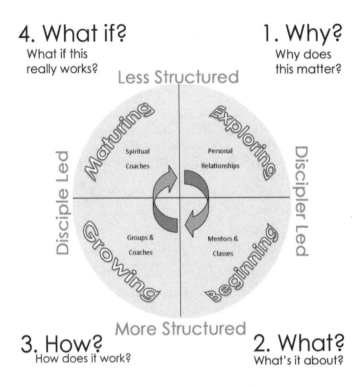

4. What if?
What if this
really works?

Less Structured

1. Why?
Why does
this matter?

Discipler Led

Disciple Led

Maturing

Exploring

Growing

Beginning

Spiritual
Coaches

Personal
Relationships

Groups &
Coaches

Mentors &
Classes

More Structured

3. How?
How does it work?

2. What?
What's it about?

The vertical axis divides the image into right and left halves. On the right side (*exploring* and *beginning* phases), the discipling that takes place is identified as Discipler Led. This is because disciples in these phases of development do not have the foundation, training, or experience to decide what would be helpful in the journey. Thinking back to the idea of stages of development (life stages), these phases would correspond to the infant and childhood stages. At these levels, people often display the following characteristics:

- There may be no commitment to being a disciple or the commitment may be fresh and untested.
- They don't know the language.
- They don't have the life skills to take care of themselves.
- They are still discovering the implications of this relationship for their world.

- People are trying out the 'relational' thing.
- They are sometimes messy.
- They don't know how to feed themselves.
- They are completely dependent upon someone who is more mature.

On the left side (*growing* and *maturing*), the disciple has developed the foundations for the journey ahead and is beginning to determine what would be most helpful in their continued development. Once again drawing a helpful comparison to the idea of life stage development, disciples on this side of the graph:

- Have the basics of the Christian life down.
- Are committed believers seeking to live a life honoring God.
- Have developed the basic skills to support the journey.
- Are seeking to continue growing their relationship with God.
- Need support as they seek to deepen certain skills.
- Are comfortable in small group and 1:1 relationships.
- Have the potential for leadership in the ministries of the church.

The horizontal axis divides the image into top and bottom halves. The bottom half (*beginning* and *growing* phases) is a time where a more structured approach—classes, small groups, mentors, coaches—are very helpful.

The top half (*exploring* and *maturing*), is the half that includes both the beginning and the end of the continuum and incorporates the times in the development process where a less structured approach is more helpful. For example, people in the *exploring* phase don't need a small group. They need a one-to-one relationship where they can ask questions and explore the faith. People in the *maturing* phase may find a partnership with a discipleship coach or a spiritual director to be helpful, but generally they have moved beyond the effectiveness of the typical class or small group.

Notice that each quadrant identifies a specific question that is being asked by those in that particular phase of development.

In the **exploring** phase, the question is "**Why**"? Why should I become a disciple? Why am I feeling this desire to be in a relationship with Jesus? Why would I want to upend my life and focus on the things of God rather than my own desires? Why would I be willing to give up the way I have been living up to now? The church needs to be ready to help people explore these kinds of questions. Often this kind of support is offered by one-on-one relationships like those provided by Faith Guides, Hospitality Angels, Mentors, or Disciplers.

In the **beginning** phase, the question is **"What"**? I have decided to become a disciple, now what do I have to do to make it happen? What does it mean to be in a relationship with God? What does life as a disciple look like? Supporting disciples in the beginning phase of development is often accomplished by classes (e.g. *Foundations: An Introduction to Spiritual Practices)* or by an introduction to Christian beliefs or a mentoring relationship.

In the **growing** phase, the question is **"How"**? How do I grow my relationship with Jesus? How do I witness, pray, reflect on Scripture, use my resources, and serve?

Supporting disciples in the growing phase is usually accomplished by one of the previously presented models of small groups. As disciples move toward the maturing phase, they often find that a partnership with a mentor or coach is very helpful. Those wrestling with the 'how' question (*growing* phase) are also at a point in the journey where they are ready for some more intensive training on putting practices into place that are representative of growing disciples:

Helping people become more generous probably means helping them learn how to handle their finances in a biblical manner. Lots of great resources are available to support this type of training.

- Helping disciples become more comfortable with building relationships outside of the church to introduce others to the love of God probably means teaching them the basics of relational evangelism and faith-sharing.

- Helping disciples discern how God has wired them for service, providing the maximum Kingdom impact and personal joy, probably means guiding them through a process of personal discovery.

- Helping disciples discover a deeper relationship with Jesus probably means introducing them to a wide variety of spiritual practices.

These and many more opportunities to provide equipping in the 'how' are ways to resource small group ministries and build growing/maturing disciples.

In the **maturing** phase, the question is **"What If"**? What if I give myself fully to this life of discipleship? What would it mean to be fully surrendered to Jesus? What difference will this make for me, my community of faith, and the community in which I live? In most cases, supporting disciples in the maturing phase requires a movement from the traditional small group focus to promoting one-on-one relationships. These are disciples with strong faith, deepening spiritual practices, and a longing to live fully into their relationship with Christ. These are also the disciples in the best position to be equipped for leadership roles in the ministry of the local congregation. Developing as leaders is a natural progression for maturing disciples. Equipping these maturing disciples to serve as mentors, coaches, small group leaders, and team leaders for ministries of the local congregation is a great blessing for both the church and the disciples themselves.

One of the lessons the church is learning again is that "one-size-fits-all" doesn't work. Even congregations like Willow Creek Community Church with its 20,000 worshipers are re-tooling from this established mindset. As noted in the *Reveal* Study:

> The Dissatisfied segment includes people from the more advanced spiritual growth segments, so they exhibit all the signs of full devotion:
>
> • Attend weekend services . . .
> • Participate in small groups . . .
> • Volunteer at church . . .
> • Serve those in need . . .
> • Tithe . . .
> • Diligent in personal efforts to grow . . .
>
> Although the Dissatisfied segment appears totally aligned with the attitudes and behaviors related to a Christ-Centered life, they still want the church to help 'keep them on track,' to hold them accountable and keep them challenged. A tool like a personal spiritual growth plan might address some of those needs. But they also seem to want a personal growth coach or spiritual mentor. That may be what would truly 'keeps them on track' and from walking out the back door. [13]

There is great value in providing one-on-one coaching, mentoring, and spiritual direction relationships if we really want the participants in our congregational life to grow as maturing disciples. People feel valued when it is clear that someone cares about their spiritual growth. Several years ago the Gallup organization published findings about engagement in faith communities in a book titled, *Growing An Engaged Church.* The big reveal was that the most engaging churches had a focus on spiritual conversations:

> People come to churches expecting to grow; it is up to church leaders to provide opportunities for growth. Beyond providing such opportunities, leaders should follow up and ask members about their experiences. . . .

> Here are items that address the issue of "How can we grow?"

> <u>In the last six months, someone in my congregation/parish has talked to me about the progress of my spiritual growth</u>. Just as members need to know the expectations of church membership, they must also know how they are progressing in meeting those expectations—particularly in the area of spiritual growth.

> Congregations are often woefully inadequate when it comes to providing feedback to members about their progress. . . . Members have no way to check their progress regarding spiritual growth because these kinds of expectations have never been clarified. . . . [14]

Perhaps an illustration by Reggie McNeal would help us to nail down the impact of what we have been describing:

> Several years ago, I joined a YMCA near my home. I met with Jason, the resident trainer who worked out of a class cubicle in the room of torture. What if, when I went to see Jason, he had challenged me to prove my commitment to the Y by getting on all those machines in the room? Further, suppose he had pulled down a picture of Mr. Universe to show me my goals and predetermined regimen. Would this have seemed strange? Of course it would have! But that's what would have happened if the YMCA operated like the program-driven church. (Actually, if the Y operated like the church, it'd bring people in once a week, feed them coffee and donuts, and let them watch Jason work out!)

> What Jason actually did was ask me simple questions: "What would you like to accomplish at the Y?" Based on my response,

he customized for me a path through that room. . . . [H]e didn't lecture me on what I needed to do. Because he invited me into the discussion, he earned my trust and made me more receptive to his advice.

Spiritual leaders, pay attention! What if we actually began to see ourselves as responsible for creating a culture where people get to participate in customizing their spiritual journeys based on their spiritual appetites and ambitions? [15]

Questions for Reflection

1. What types of relational connections does your church provide?

Maturing	
Growing	
Beginning	
Exploring	
Searching	

2. What is the framework for your small group meetings?

3. Where does 'accountable discipleship' fit into the current focus on making disciples?

4. How do those who are 'exploring' the faith, but have not yet committed, have an opportunity within your ministry context to decide if becoming a disciple is the right thing for them?

chapter four

Equipping for Transformation

Moving from the old models of Christian Education to new models of Discipleship Formation

"Do not be conformed to this world, but be transformed by the renewing of your minds, so that you may discern what is the will of God—what is good and acceptable and perfect."
–Romans 12:2

"Every one, though born of God in an instant, yea and sanctified in an instant, yet undoubtedly grows by slow degrees." –John Wesley

A New Role for Christian Ed

I do a fair amount of coaching with pastors and church leadership teams around the country. I frequently work with pastors and congregations in transformation and new church planting. One of the things we include in the covenant for the coaching relationship is that I will not tell them what to do until they have explored everything they might already know

99

to do themselves to move forward. That's because coaching is focused on 'drawing out' from the individual or team what they already know but don't know they know—dots they are in possession of but have not yet connected. Of course, sometimes a point comes in these conversations where it is clear the pastor or team simply does not know how to move forward in a positive manner. At that moment, I ask if I can switch hats and be a teacher or a consultant for a few minutes.

That's what I invite us to do now: switch hats and consider the role of Christian Education in the local congregation. Despite your years of experience in developing Christian Education curriculum and teaching Bible classes, what if there was an altogether different approach? In the previous section I made a significant distinction between the roles of discipleship and Christian Education. In no way was that meant to diminish the importance of the educational process. Christian Education, at its best, is intentionally designed to support the development of maturing disciples.

The Wesley small group at FUMC is comprised of a group of guys who, for the most part, have been active in the congregation for several years. They get together twice a month for a time of fellowship, prayer, learning, service, and accountability for their journey as disciples of Jesus. The Conference had recently provided access to the *Real Discipleship Survey* and the group had decided to each take the survey and see where they placed themselves on the continuum of maturity as disciples. Once they completed the survey and compared their results, the members of this particular group were all surprised to have placed themselves in the Beginning phase in the "Life Opening to Jesus" dimension of discipleship. The certainly didn't think of themselves as beginners—each of them had been practicing a daily devotional time for as long as they had been together—it was part of their covenant accountability! It took the survey to highlight the reality that this perfunctory daily practice had become rote. They had not really explored other ways to encounter Jesus through spiritual practices.

The group leader had a conversation with the Christian Education Director and learned that the church provided a great resource called *Companions in Christ* which explored a wide variety of spiritual practices. The group members decided that it would be beneficial for them to engage these materials, and they committed the next several months to going through this study as part of their time together. This is the role of Christian Education—to resource the development of disciples in the journey toward maturity.

In the last church I served as a 'real' pastor, I came to a breakthrough realization. For years I had done an annual stewardship focus in the fall with preaching connected to the faithful use of the resources God had provided. We even had witnesses give testimonies about the difference tithing (as a way of putting God first) had made in their lives. Yet, in this middle to upper middle class community, the giving level was for the most part around 3% or less. People were missing out on the blessings God wanted for them, and the church was limited in its ability to do effective ministry.

Then it dawned on me. It doesn't really matter how much money one makes. If we are living at the capacity of our resources and beyond, no amount of desire to be faithful stewards will be enough to become tithers. If there are no resources left after meeting our basic obligations, we simply cannot be a generous people. The problem wasn't that people didn't want to support the ministries. The problem was that they couldn't. They didn't have any margin. They didn't know how to handle their resources in a biblical manner.

So, we decided to introduce training in biblical financial management. We ended up using the Dave Ramsey resource, *Financial Peace University.* Our first group, representing about 10 families, reduced their debt over the three months of this course by about $60,000 (all combined). It was an amazing result! Other groups were formed, and then we used the materials in a large group teaching setting to introduce the concepts to the larger congregation. With no other significant changes in the life of the congregation, the giving level that first year increased by about 15%.

All the result of Christian Education.

In this part of our discussion, let's focus on what types of equipping/training might be most helpful for each of the phases of development.

In the Searching Phase

In the **searching** phase, where people outside of the church are looking for meaning in life, it is important to have disciples who are equipped to share their faith story and to be the presence of Christ in other people's lives. This is a huge gap in the educational process in most congregations.

In my research, using the *Real Discipleship Survey* with local congregations, it is not unusual to have only 1-2% of the respondents indicate that they are intentionally building relationships with people outside the church to be an expression of the love of God in their lives. In our contemporary expression of discipleship, especially in mainline denominations, it seems that we rarely even tell people that this is part of what it means to be a disciple of Jesus. The Great Commission, "Go…make disciples," is relegated to a committee in the church rather than being seen as part and parcel of the work of discipleship expected of every person in the congregation. Having the confidence to practice Incarnational Hospitality (being the presence of

Christ in someone's life) and to share one's faith story (our own personal experiences with Jesus) should be something that is developed as we practice on each other, honing our skills in the safe environment of Christian community.

But we have to teach people how to do this.

In a resource called *Connect,* participants are equipped to:

- Build relationships with people that move beyond 'friends' on Facebook that they never meet.
- Share their faith stories in a variety of ways.
- Build a personal testimony.
- Connect with their neighbors.
- Leverage their circle of influence.
- Engage their communities.
- Develop relationships through service. [1]

In a book titled, *Get Their Name,* Bob Farr, Kay Kotan, and Doug Anderson provide a great framework for building the development of faith-sharing skills into the existing infrastructure of the small group and worship ministries of the church. They liken the process of learning to share our faith to the progression from elementary school, to middle school, to high school and finally to college:

- Elementary school focus: practicing relational evangelism through service connected with sharing the Good News.
- Middle school focus: practicing relational evangelism through sharing our faith stories in small groups.
- High school focus: practicing faith sharing through witnesses/testimony in worship services.
- College focus: sharing our faith/inviting people to worship through connections beyond the local church. [2]

You may have noticed that the things we have been talking about here are reflective of the **maturing** phase in the Life of Hospitality dimension discussed earlier in this book. This is where we intentionally build relationships with people so that they may discover the love of Christ for themselves. We'll come back to this later. I want to emphasize something that is very important for our church members to understand, and at the same time I want to debunk a myth that has a very strong hold on our churches. This myth is the mindset that the average disciple, particularly if they are just beginning the journey, does not know enough to be an effective witness to those outside the church.

It has been my experience that people are less interested in deep theological knowledge and advanced exegesis of Scriptures—I can say this in Greek!—than they are in your personal experience of Jesus at work in your life. I would go so far as to say that, in actuality, those who are beginning the journey are some of the best witnesses to the faith. There is a freshness and an enthusiasm for what they are experiencing that is captivating. From the very beginning of the journey, we ought to be setting expectations and encouraging people to share their faith.

Recently, a young man named Blake showed up on the doorstep of our church. He had lost his job (and thus his car) and was feeling adrift, and had ridden his bike five miles to check out our church (that's how desperate he was to find meaning and connection somewhere—anywhere). And he did. He was welcomed with open arms and invited into worship without expectations, and this outpouring of grace gave him a new purpose and sense of worth. It is true that he did not yet know much about the Bible, and he was perplexed whenever we started absent-mindedly tossing around churchy terms likes "sanctification," but he loved to tell his story. And people loved to hear it, because it was full of enthusiasm and authenticity.

Such stories of God's work in the world have always had great power, and it is important to note that Christian Education is not limited to the classroom. When we let go of the old restrictive model for how to nurture disciples, we find that worship, for instance, becomes a training ground (just as much as the classroom) for people learning how to live more fully into the life God offers, including "helping to make other disciples." In this particular example, the testimonies offered in worship not only witness to the ways God is at work in the community of faith. They invite those hearing the testimony to consider and even become aware of how God is at work in their lives. They also offer a model for the worshipers about how to share their stories.

Tied very closely to the equipping of disciples to share their faith stories is providing opportunities for disciples to be the presence of Christ in people's lives through service. Professor and author, Lovett Weems, notes that "we must earn the right to be heard." Perhaps the old adage is not so far off: People want to know how much we care before they care how much we know.

In a world where a vast majority of people view the church as irrelevant to their lives, the practice of serving others and making a difference in our communities is how we earn the right to be heard. When you take care of a neighbor recovering from an illness or injury, when you give your time teaching a student how to read or helping a child from another country learn our language, or when you coach the local soccer team, you are serving in a way that opens the door to naturally evolving conversations about why you do what you do. Notice that this is different from painting picnic tables at the school or even providing backpacks. This is service that is done in a way that allows you to build relationships. It is service that provides the opportunity to share our stories and invite people to discover God's love for them.

In the first church I served in the Florida Conference, we offered a Thursday night meal, called Manna Kitchen, for the homeless and lonely and hungry in the community. When we first started the ministry, our leadership team made a commitment to come and serve in the Manna Kitchen. After just a few weeks it became clear that there were plenty of people from the church who would like to help, and serving was an easy way to engage them. It was also clear that we were missing an opportunity. While we got to know some of the people's names and certainly got to greet everyone as they came to eat, we didn't have an opportunity to really get to know them. So the leadership team committed to coming and eating with the community while other church members served the meal.

It was amazing! We got to meet some incredible people. We got to hear their stories. They got to hear ours. Out of these conversations relationships were built, and God's love was experienced. Some of the people who came to eat began to come to other activities—even worship! All because we took the opportunity to build relationships. Alan Hirsch calls this the distinction between Presence and Proximity. When we are present, we are building the relationships, hanging out with people Jesus loves. In proximity we are involved in their lives and available to them in whatever they encounter.

In the Exploring Phase

Louie Giglio, contemporary Christian songwriter, shares the following story from his early life working as a photocopy assistant in the Centers for Disease Control:

> But God was doing a lot in my heart in those days and the job became something more. I'm not trying to overspiritualize what happened (we didn't end up having a revival in the library), but by God's grace I was able to turn that copy room into a place I loved.
>
> For one thing, I wanted to be the best copier on earth, never leaving work until every waiting article was produced . . . something

that often required improvements in my technique, speed, and productivity. I would not be denied.

But also, this job gave me lots of time to hang out with God. Photocopying, though manually intensive, doesn't overly deplete the brain. Which left lots of time for thoughts of God. Time to talk to Him. Time to worship. Time to listen. Time to pray.

Everyone working there knew I was a believer, but they weren't exactly asking me to lead a Bible study or talk about the Savior. My witness was my work . . . and work was my worship. The way I did my work was possibly even more significant than anything I could do or say.

I became, to put it modestly, the master copier. And you know what I think? I think the way I did my work reflected something good about the character of God. [3]

So, imagine for a moment, that someone interacting with Louie became intrigued with the way he did life. Obviously there was something different about him. They were so curious that they asked him about where he went to church. Then one day they showed up to see if the church was the kind of place that created people like Louie.

In the **exploring** phase, people from outside the church are coming to the church—sometimes to worship, sometimes to neighborhood gatherings, and sometimes to help serve the community. They are checking out the church. They may have met someone like you, and they want to see if the church actually produces disciples that do life the way you do. Or perhaps they were impressed with a service activity your church was involved in and are checking to see if this is a strong focus.

People in the **exploring** phase have lots of questions. There are lots of people who have grown up never being exposed to Christianity, and they don't really know what it means to be a Christian. They have heard (and seen, especially on TV and in movies) all the negative stuff about Christians, so they don't really get the 'abundant life' that we talk about. They need information and insight, but what explorers don't need is a class!

For these explorers, at this point in their journey, it is most helpful for them to have guides from the congregation who serve in some kind of one-to-one relationship where questions can be answered, concerns explored, and faith shared. These persons don't need to be experts in theology, biblical exegesis, or doctrines of the church. They can be most helpful when they answer questions with these kinds of responses: "Here's what I have discovered in my relationship," and "I'm not sure I know the answer to that, but we can sure find someone who does." Perhaps more (much more) important than being able to answer every question is the ability to accept the person where they are and build a sense of trust in the relationship.

Beyond the availability of these kinds of personal connections, it is very important that the worship service reflects the heart of the congregation. For example, if the congregation is committed to making a difference in the community through acts of service, it is helpful for this to be communicated through witnesses or testimonies. In a culture where so many don't feel like the church is relevant to their lives, it is critical that the message presented be applicable to real life.

Churches are boldly seeking creative ways to communicate the Gospel message. For example, one pastor is leading a "Theology in a Pub" event each month to have a place people can invite their friends where it is a non-threatening atmosphere and an open forum for asking whatever questions people have.

In the Beginning Phase

Life seemed to be falling apart for Sally. Her marriage of just a couple of years had just disintegrated, and she now had complete responsibility for an infant and no significant means of support. A friend had suggested that she might find support through a local church. So Sally showed up in worship for the first time and heard an amazing message about there being nothing that can separate us from the love of God for us in Christ Jesus. Tears were flowing as she looked around the room at people who obviously cared a great deal about each other. It had been a while since she felt that kind of caring in her life.

At the end of the service the pastor issued an invitation for those who had not ever asked Jesus to be part of their lives and who longed for an experience of God's love. Sally went forward, carrying her infant daughter. It was one of the most powerful moments of her life. She couldn't wait to experience the love so obviously represented in the lives of those in the room and in the community as a whole.

So now what?

Sally had been prayed for. She had made a confession of faith. The closing hymn had been sung and the benediction offered. A couple of people hugged Sally and welcomed her to the community. And then everybody filed out, and Sally was left with this profound experience and a lot of confusion about what was next for her life. How does she begin to understand who this God really is and the power of the relationship she has begun? How does she begin to live life in such a way that she encounters God regularly? Who will help her find her way?

In the **beginning** phase of development, the greatest need of the disciple is to know what they need to know and what they need to do to begin a journey as a disciple. In my work with churches this is often a pretty big gap in the Christian education offerings.

Almost without question, there are some expectations that we as leaders have of those beginning the journey. For example, we (the church/pastors/directors of education) want people to:

- Pray.
- Read their Bibles.
- Live in authentic relationships.
- Have a devotional time.
- Participate in worship (personal/corporate).
- Serve others.
- Use their resources in ways that honor God.
- Witness to their faith.

But where do people learn to do these things? We seem to think they will absorb them by just sitting in the pews in worship on Sundays. Disciples have to be taught how to live out these spiritual practices. In my work with churches it is rare that any intentional training is offered at this phase of development—usually 10% or less of churches have some kind of foundational classes. Consequently, I began to recommend that this kind of focus be built into the discipling process. To my surprise, pastors started contacting me and asking about where to find a good resource. I went looking and found all the information, of course, but you had to have several books to cover all the themes. To support the discipling process at this level I ended up writing a book called *Foundations: An Introduction to Spiritual Practices.* To my surprise, even though the book was intended for beginning disciples, churches began to have long-term church members wanting this kind of training as well (apparently they weren't getting it by osmosis). Several churches have done church-wide studies with these materials, and others are building it in to their new member process.

It also cannot be overstated that the efficacy of the training provided in this phase is dependent on a solid theological understanding. Weak beliefs tend to limit our development as disciples. A couple of good resources for this include:

- *Alpha Course* by Nicky Gumble. [4]
- *Beginnings* by Andy Langford and Mark Rails. [5]

Another great resource for equipping disciples at this level of development is the Emmaus Walk. In a concentrated weekend experience disciples are exposed to strong theological understandings and introduced to a wide variety of spiritual practices.

Of course, our strongest and most frequent venue for training disciples is during worship services, and we so often miss this wonderful opportunity. For example, where do people learn how to pray? Over the years of my ministry, it was a standard practice for me to offer an annual class on prayer. I would like to say that this class participation was so strong that it was 'standing room only.' Unfortunately, a very small percentage of people took me up on this opportunity—about five from a congregation of 650+. And these were my prayer warriors! They were the ones I was already turning to when I needed someone to pray for a special need in my life or ministry.

So where were the rest of the people learning how to pray? Probably by listening to the pastoral/corporate prayers offered in worship or at the beginnings of gatherings.

Wanting to strengthen the prayer life of the congregation, we began to do a monthly focus on a prayer model. It would go something like this:

- Today we are going to offer the pastoral prayer using the framework of the ACTS model of prayer.
- You will find the components of this model described in your bulletin so that you can follow along and see how we follow this model.
- When you leave worship today, we encourage you to take your bulletin with you and try the ACTS model for your prayer time during the next week.

The same types of things can be done with introducing Scripture study methods, introducing spiritual practices like guided meditations or breath prayers. For example, instead of just reading the Scriptures to people in worship, what if we invited them to take out their Bibles (or smartphones with a Bible app) and engage two to three people around them by reading through the text being used for worship that day and responding to three questions:

- What does this text tell us about God?
- What does this text tell us about humankind?
- What does this text tell us about our relationship with God?

This simple theological Bible study, often used in courses like *Disciple*, is a great way to resource participants in worship for studying Scripture in their personal devotional times. There are dozens of easy tools like this that could be incorporated into the worship experience.

In the Growing Phase

Tim is a growing disciple of Jesus Christ. He has been very active in his church for the past several years. He is regular in worship, gives proportionately, helps out around the church, is part of a small group, and has a daily devotional time with God. Yet something seems to be missing.

Tim has met you and is intrigued. To him, you seem to have a direct line to God. It's deeper and different than his own experience. It's like you always know what God wants for your life. You are clear about how God has called you to serve. Sharing your faith story just seems to come naturally for you. And you tithe and yet seem to have plenty of resources to enjoy life. It's almost as if God speaks to you. And Tim wants that for himself. He wants to BE like that. He's been doing the daily devotional reading that he was encouraged to do in the *Foundations* class. He prays (although mostly through 'bullet point prayers'). He is reading through the Bible in a year. But Tim knows there is more to this life as a disciple. He sees it in you and others like you. So Tim is asking, "How do I get that?" At this point in the journey Tim is ready for more and wants to know "how."

- How do I give myself more completely in worship to God?
- How do I reflect on Scripture in a way that God can speak into my life?
- How do I pray so that I might be more open to the presence of God in the moment? And the rest of the day?
- How do I know how God has wired me to serve so that others are blessed and I am fulfilled?
- How do I use the resources God has provided to me in ways that honor God?
- How do I build relationships with people beyond the church so that I can be a witness of God's love for them?

- How do I share the story about God at work in my life and the difference that has made?
- How do I develop other spiritual practices that will help me to be aware of God in the moment and God present throughout the rest of my day and week?

In the **growing** phase of development, disciples are discovering **how** to do life in a way that honors God. They have built the foundations of personal devotional times, have begun to consider how they use resources, and perhaps are even inviting others to church. But they know there is something more to this life in Christ Jesus. Growing disciples have a good sense of what it is that God wants for their lives. The question becomes how to get there.

This phase of development needs to be very focused on helping disciples discover how to live in ways that honor God. Christian Education can play a large role in helping this happen, but it needs to move away from offering a curriculum focused solely on Bible study opportunities. The following are some themes that desperately need to be addressed in growing disciples, as well as some suggestions for supporting those areas of growth. This needs to be a very intentional process with the expectation that all disciples will eventually participate in these areas of spiritual growth:

A Life of Worship: Equipping in this area of discipleship includes the focus on growing a heart for worship and a lifestyle of worship.
    Suggested Resources:

- *The Unquenchable Worshipper,* by Matt Redman. [6]
- *Worship His Majesty,* by Jack Hayford. [7]

A Life of Hospitality: Equipping in this area of discipleship includes the development of interpersonal relationships, dealing with conflict, faith-sharing, and incarnational hospitality.
    Suggested resources:

- *Making Room.* [8]
- *Get Their Name.* [9]
- *Peace Makers Conflict Study.* [10]
- *Authentic Community.* [11]
- *Connect.* [12]

A Life Opening to Jesus: Equipping in this area of discipleship includes the development of spiritual practices, moving beyond the basics to include the disciplines of meditation, solitude, praying the Scriptures, fasting, and celebration.

Suggested resources:

- *Companions in Christ.* [13]
- *Prayer* by Richard Foster. [14]

A Life Obeying Jesus: Equipping in this area of discipleship includes reflection on Scripture, the application of Scripture to life, journaling, mentoring, and discipleship coaching.

Suggested resources:

- *A Reflective Life*, Ken Gire. [15]
- *Discipleship Coaching Training* (CLTI). [16]

A Life of Service: Equipping in this area of discipleship includes the discernment of how God has 'wired' people for service: spiritual gifts, passions, personality, abilities/talents, and life experiences.

Suggested resources:

- *SHAPE* – Eric Reese. [17]
- *PLACE.* [18]

A Life of Generosity: Equipping in this area of discipleship includes helping disciples understand basic biblical principles of financial management, building in financial margins, and giving proportionately/tithing.

Suggested resources:

- *Enough* by Adam Hamilton. [19]
- *Financial Peace University.* [20]

Rather than standard Christian Education programs (such as the classes listed previously) being the mainstay of the discipling process at this point, they instead provide a supporting role. I would suggest that an expectation be set that all disciples would participate in at least one of the classes from each category as part of their ongoing development. The classes might be scheduled over the course of a year so that people could take them at their convenience, or even in an online or interactive format.

The classes may be provided in a format so that the facilitator of an existing small group could lead the discussions (most are available in a DVD supported format or as a book study). Existing small groups could use the courses to supplement their other activities based on the needs of the small group members. Or they might be offered as stand-alone courses that people could engage when they are ready. For example, the flow of a Christian Education cycle at a local church might look something like this:

Year	Fall	Winter	Spring	Summer
1	Beginning: *The Disciple's Path* Growing: *Disciple Bible Study* Maturing: *Christian Mentoring Training*	Beginning: *Connect* Growing: *Disciple Bible Study* Maturing: *Discipleship Coaching Training*	Beginning: *Foundations* Growing: *Disciple Bible Study* Maturing: *Group facilitation training (small group/ teams)*	*SHAPE with mission exploration opportunities*
2	Beginning: *Beginnings* Growing: *Financial Peace University* Maturing: *Basic Leadership Skills Training*	Beginning: *Connect* Growing: *How to Study the Bible* Maturing: *Building Personal Development Plans/ Ministry Action Plans*	Beginning: *Foundations* Growing: *Authentic Community* Maturing: *Team Building Skills*	*Community Service Opportunities with Debrief*

3	Beginning: The Disciple's Path	Beginning: Connect	Beginning: Foundations	Community Partnership Opportunities with Debrief
	Growing: Making Peace - Dealing with Conflict	Growing: Celebration of Discipline	Growing: Worship – Small group study	
	Maturing: Strategic Planning	Maturing: Project Management	Maturing: Understand- ing the Com- munity	

Again, just as in the discussions of previous phases, don't miss the potential impact of the regular worship experience as part of the equipping. For example, in introducing the offering time, make strong, clear connections between the giving and the difference that is being made in third world nations as people are supported in recovery from typhoons or fed in times of famine. Use testimonies and witnessing to communicate the impact being a blessing to others has made or the difference the giving has made in someone's life.

Help people see their giving as an act of worship!

In the Maturing Phase

In the **maturing** phase, the equipping for discipleship is much less focused on educational classes and much more focused on the experiential. Rather than a class about the practice of meditation, what if you offered a spiritual formation retreat that included the actual experience of meditation and other spiritual practices.

There is still, however, a role for Christian education in this phase as it relates to leadership development. At this level in the discipleship journey, disciples usually find the growth in their spiritual lives to be related to participation in a partnership (coaching, mentoring, spiritual direction). This can also be true in leadership development as well—and all churches need to be constantly developing disciples who are also strong leaders. There are some specific leadership skills that can be taught that are helpful in preparing disciples for roles in congregational leadership. It is hoped at this level that these maturing disciples would be thinking beyond their own internal growth and seeking opportunities to lead others toward maturity and congregations toward greater effectiveness in ministry.

Some suggestions for training include:

- *Discipleship Coaching Training:* equipping coaches in local congregations to provide partnerships with growing disciples seeking to move toward maturity in the discipleship journey. (For more information, go to www.em3coaching.com.)

- *Coaching for Leadership Training:* equipping leaders in the local congregation to use basic coaching skills and models to support their ministries. Designed to equip leaders for a 'coach approach' to leadership.

- *Facilitation Skills Training:* equipping leaders to effectively facilitate deliberations and decision-making for teams, committees, and staff. (For more information, go to www.CLTI.com at the leadership tab).

The Link Between Relationships and Learning

While it is **good** to have a solid Christian Education Program, it is **GREAT** to have a solid process for intentional discipleship supported by a solid Christian Education Program. So, in the words of Jim Collins, let's move from **good** to **GREAT!** The key factor in this shift from good to great is relationships. In the previous chapter we discussed a wide variety of relationships. No church (or at least no church I can imagine) will utilize all of these types of relationships. They were shared to show the breadth of possibilities.

I hope it was also clear that an effective process for discipleship will need to use more than one of these types of relationships. Let's go back to the Discipleship Cycle graphic:

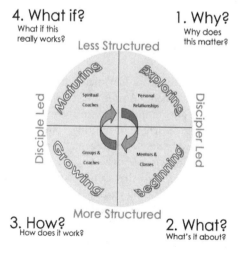

Note that each of the quadrants indicates the kind of relationships that are probably most helpful at this phase of development. For example:

Exploring Phase: A one-on-one personal relationship is the most helpful format in this phase. People need an opportunity to process what they are experiencing and explore what that might mean for their lives. They are definitely not ready for a standard class or the typical small group experience.

Beginning Phase: This is where people are learning what it means to be a disciple of Jesus. They are getting the language down. They are developing foundational holy habits. They are getting introduced to some basic understandings about God. A class works really well at this level of development. It is not intimidating. Everybody is basically at the same level of experience. They are not expected to know anything.

Growing Phase: This level of development is where the small group is most effective. But I am not talking about a Bible study group or a topical study group or even a designated organizational group (e.g. United Methodist Women in the Methodist tradition). I am talking about a group that has committed to do life together and hold each other accountable in the journey toward maturity as disciples of Jesus.

Examples of these types of groups from our previous discussion include:

- 3 – B Groups.
- Wesley Fellowship Groups.
- Covenant Discipleship Groups.

But they can be ANY kind of group that agrees to certain growth standards (even a Bible study group). The key to growth in this phase is that people are holding one another accountable. Little progress is made when someone attends a class on biblical principles of financial management but never applies any of the principles to their own personal situation. It doesn't do much good to study about the Bible if what we have processed on an intellectual level has not been applied to our personal lives. It isn't much help to study a variety of spiritual practices and then never practice any of them.

The accountability of a small group, or discipleship coach, or mentor, or spiritual director is the leverage point for movement toward maturity as a disciple of Jesus. Somebody needs to be having these conversations.

Maturing Phase: For those reaching this level of development, the traditional models of small groups (even those presented here) tend to lose their effectiveness as a discipling tool. You begin to think, "I really love this bunch of guys, but I'm not really growing anymore." And then it gets translated, "I really love this church but I'm not really getting fed here anymore."

It's exactly the same thing Willow Creek Community Church discovered as it reflected on the "Dissatisfied" group in its infamous survey. They were the most mature. And they had reached a point where the structures of the small group were no longer meeting their needs (even though Willow Creek has an amazing small group ministry). It was time for something more personal. Something more focused. It was time for a discipleship coach, a mentor, or a spiritual director.

The following graphic is designed to help you see the big picture for the development of maturing disciples in your setting:

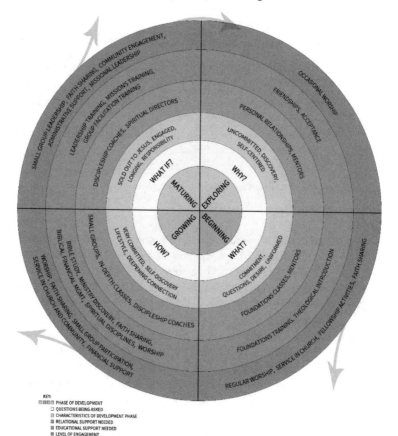

As you work your way from the inside out on this graphic, you will find:

- Level 1 identifies the four phases of development.
- Level 2 reminds you of the question each phase is asking.
- Level 3 describes the basic characteristics of disciples in each phase of development.
- Level 4 identifies the types of relationships that are most helpful for each phase.
- Level 5 provides suggestions for types of Christian education support.
- Level 6 provides insights into the level of engagement/involvement the church can expect from each phase of development.

Note that there are four arrows growing outward from the graphic. The first three of these remind us that each of those phases of development encourages us to be moving out into the community, building relationships, being Christ in people's lives, and inviting people to discover God's love for themselves. The fourth arrow indicates that this phase (maturing) is also where disciples are equipped to support the development of those in earlier phases of development.

Moving from the Random to the Purposeful

It seems that for most of the congregations I work with, the Christian education offerings have been basically random. By this I mean that they have not been thought through in terms of a process with an end goal in mind. Cindy comes to the Christian Education Director and asks if a course could be offered around the new book she is reading. She says it is a really good read and has provoked her to think deeply about her own life and the possibility for life in the years to come. It's a book called *The Secret*.

You politely thank Cindy for her interest but note that the book, while it includes some interesting ideas, is not really suitable for a Christian Education offering. In fact, there's nothing Christian about it. That one was pretty easy. But the next day, Joe shows up, and Joe has found what he considers to be a great study on the book of John. You already offer a Bible study on John, but Joe is so excited that you include the class since he has agreed to teach it. This is ad hoc decision making, with little or no thought given to the goal of a strategic plan for the ultimate outcome of producing mature disciples of Jesus.

What if, instead of random offerings selected from the newest popular speakers from around the country, the church were more intentional?

What if we knew where the gaps were in creating maturing disciples, and we planned educational support to meet the identified needs? Referring back to our hypothetical church and the *Real Discipleship Survey*, the final results show a matrix of the dimensions of discipleship and where the congregants fall in the different phases of maturity within each dimension. A graphic summary looks like this:

	Exploring	Beginning	Growing	Maturing
A Life of Worship	0%	26%	47%	26%
A Life of Hospitality	1%	29%	56%	1%
A Life Open to Jesus	15%	21%	38%	26%
A Life Obeying Jesus	1%	56%	29%	1%
A Life of Service	18%	32%	18%	32%
A Life of Generosity	1%	23%	20%	44%

Having a resource like this could give some insight into starting points. For example:

- In **A Life of Hospitality** only 1% (not uncommon) of participants place themselves in the maturing phase. This is a strong indicator that this congregation has not placed an emphasis on incarnational hospitality—building relationships with those outside the church to be an expression of God's love to them. It is likely that they don't know how to build relationships with the unchurched, are not aware of the many opportunities to engage others, and wouldn't have a clue about how to share their own personal story or testimony.

This would be a good starting point.

- In **A Life Obeying Jesus,** again only 1% of participants place themselves in the maturing phase. This is a strong indicator that this congregation has not communicated an expectation that every disciple is to be discipling someone else. It is likely they wouldn't know how to go about doing this.

This, too, would be an excellent starting point.

- In **A Life Opening to Jesus** only about a quarter of participants indicated they were at the maturing phase. The vast majority of participants are still dependent upon the church to provide for their spiritual development. Equipping them with tools for reflecting on Scripture and practicing spiritual disciplines would be a good start in moving things forward. Providing coaches would bring exponential growth.

Questions for Reflection

1. How intentional is your congregation about engaging disciples in Christian Education experiences moving toward a clear goal?

2. How does your congregation encourage the development of basic spiritual practices for new believers?

3. What training do you provide for development in:

   - Hospitality?

   - Worship?

   - Spiritual Practices?

   - Generosity?

   - Service?

   - Reflection on Scripture?

chapter five

Putting the Pieces Together

Charting a navigable path to discipleship

"And they devoted themselves to the apostles' teaching and the fellowship, to the breaking of bread and the prayers." –Acts 2:42

"God has entrusted us with his most precious treasure—people. He asks us to shepherd and mold them into strong disciples, with brave faith and good character. " –John Ortberg

GOD'S GRACE AT WORK WITHIN US

| SEARCHING for Meaning | EXPLORING Christ's Way | BEGINNING New Life In Christ | GROWING Our Walk In Christ | MATURING Our Walk In Christ |

PREVENIENT GRACE   JUSTIFYING GRACE   SANCTIFYING GRACE

In previous chapters, we have looked at how the phases of discipleship growth parallel the physical and mental development of all humans. Growth as a disciple, however, is not an autonomous process that organically proceeds heedless of conscious management on our part. Growth as a follower of Jesus Christ is a matter of will, decision, and effort.

We have previously discussed some of the relational infrastructure that is helpful to facilitate this growth, and we have explored some of the educational support that equips disciples to make life transformation happen. But we have talked about all of this in language that makes it seem like 'making disciples' is something WE (the church) do. This is only natural since we have denominational mission statements like:

> *Make disciples of Jesus Christ for the transformation of the world.*
>
> —*The United Methodist Book of Discipline*

And even the words of Jesus in the Great Commission:

> *"Go, therefore, and make disciples . . . baptizing them . . . and teaching them. . . ."*
>
> —Matthew 28: 19-20 (NRSV)

However, the reality is that we (the church) do not really make disciples. God makes disciples. We provide the framework and the opportunities and the educational resources to support what God is doing. But it is God who makes disciples. It is God at work through Prevenient Grace—the working of the Spirit of God to woo us, draw us in, invite us—that introduces us to the relationship of being a disciple. It is God at work through Justifying Grace—the working of the Spirit of God to place us in a relationship where we are justified (made right with God) that we experience imputed righteousness (God's choice to see us as righteous). And it is God at work through Sanctifying Grace—the working of the Spirit of God in our lives to impart (make actual) the righteousness of Christ—through which we journey toward 'Christian Perfection' or completeness.

With that clarified (and in the spirit of Paul's admonition to "work out your salvation"), there is much we as the church can and should do to make the pathway to maturity as a disciple as navigable as possible. Throughout history there have been a few processes that stand out as exceptional.

Biblical Models of Discipleship

The Jesus Approach

One of the best descriptions of this approach to discipleship is a video segment by Rob Bell. It is part of the Nooma Series and is entitled "Dust." You can watch this video on YouTube by searching the site for "rob bell, dust." While you may or may not agree completely with Bell's theology, this video highlights a model of discipleship practiced in the time of Jesus that changed the world as it was known.

The educational system for Jewish children focused on the memorization of scriptures, with greater and greater portions of Scripture memorized as students advanced into their teenage years. At that point most of these students would return to learning a trade by working in the family business. A select few, those with the clearest aptitude for this kind of training, would apply to be a disciple of a rabbi (teacher). The rabbi would have conversations with them inspired by the Scriptures and the interpretation of the Scriptures known as the Midrash. If the student were exceptional, and the rabbi thought they had potential, they would advance further. The best of the best were selected to be disciples. These students would leave their homes, their families, and their communities to follow the rabbi. Wherever the rabbi went and whatever the rabbi did, the students would follow closely in the rabbi's footsteps, taking on the character and developing the skills of the rabbi.

Hence, a saying of blessing was developed for these students: "May you be covered in the dust of your rabbi."

Jesus followed this pattern for making disciples with one very important distinction. The people he invited to be disciples had already returned to their families and were already engaged in the family trade by the time Jesus came along and said, "Come, follow me." The implication is clear. You don't have to be the best of the best in academic performance. We can be a disciple of Jesus when the heart is in the right place. It is a possibility for each and every one of us to become like Jesus and to do the things Jesus did. But this doesn't happen by accident. Greg Ogden, in *Transforming Discipleship,* examines the discipleship approach of Jesus. The following graphic summarizes that process: [1]

	Pre disciple (Seeking)	Phase I (Exploring)	Phase II (Beginning)	Phase III (Growing)	Phase IV (Maturing)
Jesus' Role	Inviter	Living Example	Provocative Teacher	Supportive Coach	Ultimate Delegator
The Disciples' Role	Seekers	Observers & Imitators	Students & Questioners	Short Term Missionaries	Apostles
Readiness Level	Hungry to know about Messiah	Ready to observe who Jesus is	Ready to interact & identify with Jesus	Ready to test the authority of Jesus	Ready to assume full responsibility
Key Question	Is Jesus Messiah?	Is Jesus Messiah?	What is the cost of following Jesus?	Will the power of Jesus work in me?	Will I give my life to the disciple making mission?

You will note that Ogden's framework is similar to the phases of development highlighted in our earlier chapters. He identifies five phases of development, but his descriptions are a bit more generic than the ones we developed, so I have included our familiar terminology in parentheses under his phases on the graphic. Let's consider the various components of this approach:

- *The Disciples' role:* Notice the movement from the left side of the graphic to the right as disciples move from checking out what it means to be a disciple (observers and imitators) to learning what to do as disciples (students) to beginning to develop the how of applying this new lifestyle (short term missionaries) to fully representing Christ to the world (apostles). It is a shift from us (and our development) to a focus on the world and how we can make a difference in it—very similar to the *Real Discipleship* matrix presented previously.

- *Jesus' role:* In a fashion similar to considering the role of the church in making disciples, Jesus starts out as Inviter (incarnational hospitality), moves to being the Example (the witness of the church), becomes the Teacher (providing training), moves to being the Supportive Coach (helps disciples see how to live out their calling), and then becomes Delegator (sending maturing disciples out to be Christ in the world).

- Even the questions Ogden identifies are similar to concepts we have previously considered:
  - o Why? (Is Jesus the Messiah?)
  - o What? (What is the cost?)
  - o How? (Will the power of Jesus work in me?)
  - o What if? (Will I give my life to the disciple making mission?)

Paul's Approach

Ogden identifies a different but very similar approach used by the Apostle Paul and represented in the following graphic: [2]

The Apostle Paul's Process

Life Stage	Life Stage Role	Disciples Role	Paul's Role
Infancy	Modeling and direction	Imitation	Model
Childhood	Unconditional love and protection	Identification	Hero
Adolescence	Increased freedom and identity formation	Exhortation	Coach
Adulthood	Mutuality and reciprocity	Participation	Peer

Adapted from *Transforming Discipleship*, Greg Ogden

Ogden shows how Paul emulates Jesus' example. Note in particular:

- *The Disciples' role:* Starting with imitation (the infancy phase), the disciples watch and learn from those who are more mature; then they move to identification (the childhood phase) where they begin to form life around teachings; they grow from there to exhortation (the adolescence phase), in which the disciples are encouraged and given freedom to use what they are becoming; and ultimately they arrive at participation (the adulthood phase) in which the disciples realize their goal of full partnership in building the kingdom

- *Paul's role:* Paul starts out as a model, moves to hero (in the sense of being looked up to), serves as coach (supporting the disciples as they serve), and ultimately becomes a peer to his fellow, fully engaged disciples.

The Early Church's Approach

In Christianity during the first couple of centuries, there were very clear expectations and a three-year process of development/probation period for those being admitted into the church as disciples of Jesus Christ   This included instruction by a mentor for about two years which was focused around the materials in the *Didache* (a discipleship program which eventually became known as *The Training of the Lord through the Twelve Apostles to the Gentiles*). [3]

The process for admission into the Christian community had several steps:

- Recommendation of a present member vouching for authenticity of faith.
- Three-year probation period.
- Doctrinal and moral training (during three year probation).
- Examination of knowledge and conduct.
- Training in the Scriptures.
- Initiation into spiritual practices.
- Baptism.
- Acceptance into the community and celebration of Holy Communion.

Can you imagine a church that required a three-year process for membership in our culture today?

I work with a fair number of churches that have no process at all. At the end of worship an invitation is extended: "If you would like to join this congregation today, simply come forward during our closing hymn." And then they are asked to respond to the membership vows. This is a reasonable approach if your goal is to get members on the rolls and have your church look really healthy and relevant for those who admire spreadsheets. It is not a great metric for measurement if your goal is making disciples.

It is a blind invitation—open and accessible, true, but generic in the sense that it does not meet the person with a sense of guiding them on their highly personal journey of discipleship. You know nothing about the man or woman who steps forward on the seventh verse of "Just As I Am." You don't know if they have been baptized. You don't know if they have been a member of a church somewhere else, where they are on the pathway to maturity as a disciple, or what level of commitment they have to the life and ministry of your local congregation.

The Early Methodists' Discipleship Model

Several years ago, Eric Geiger (co-author of the book, *Simple Church)* was presenting a series of workshops in the Florida Conference of the United Methodist Church around the *Simple Church* themes. As a Conference staff person, I had the responsibility of getting Eric to the locations where he would be speaking. As we were driving into Gainesville for an event, Eric turned to me and asked the question: "Phil, I just have one question. What's wrong with you people?"

My initial response was that he would have to be more specific. I could think of a lot of answers to that question. Then he said: "I work with pastors and church leaders from a wide variety of tribes [denomination/ non-denominational traditions]. All of them are using the best discipleship process since the time of Jesus—the one developed by John Wesley and the early Methodists. Everybody, that is, but the Methodists. What's wrong with you people?"

I didn't have an answer.

What was so special about the discipleship approach of John Wesley? The following graphic provides insight:

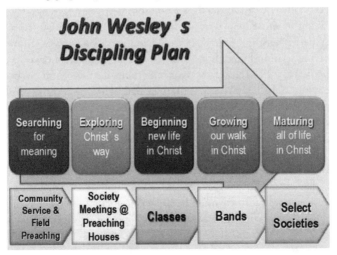

John Wesley and the early Methodists first and foremost had a heart for the community—for people outside the church. The covenant they ascribed to included serving people in some way each week. The Methodist preachers were known for bringing the message of the gospel to those outside of the church, preaching at the mines and the inner cities and even in cemeteries. John Wesley penned the words in his journal that became a theme of his ministry and the theme of Methodism as the movement grew. He wrote, "I look upon all the world as my parish. [It is] my bounden duty to declare to all who are willing to hear, the glad tidings of salvation." [4]

People were drawn to the gospel of Christ through the lives of those called Methodists (which was, by the way, a derogatory designation critiquing the strong focus on *methods*, such as committing to serve someone each week, studying the Scriptures every day, and praying for family and friends). The Methodists cared for the sick, visited those in prison, fed the hungry, and clothed the poor. It seems there was something about being the witness of Christ in the world that drew people to the love of Jesus for themselves. Some of the people who experienced God's grace through their interactions with these so-called Methodists asked about how they could learn more. At this point in their spiritual journey, they were invited to Wesley's Society Meeting.

A Society Meeting had all the elements of what we would call a worship service today. There were prayers and hymns and Scripture readings and sermons and the sacrament of communion and altar calls. The underlying message of the teaching time was 'the desire to flee from the wrath to come.' It was an invitation to discipleship framed in a rather negative context which would not be well received in contemporary culture. But it was culturally relevant for its time, and thus effective, in Wesley's day.

Some of those who were drawn to Society Meetings by the acts of mercy performed by Methodists would inquire about how to move into this saving relationship with Jesus Christ and, in particular, how to become Methodists as well. The answer went something like this: "You can become a Methodist only if you will commit to be part of a Class Meeting. You can become a Christian by going to church and giving your life to Christ. But to be a Methodist you have to join a Class Meeting." The Class Meeting was where one learned how to live as a disciple of Jesus Christ.

The Class Meeting was not just informational. It was transformational. Based on my research, this is how I envision the class meetings of the time. Each 'class' was led by a Class Leader—a maturing disciple of Jesus Christ. The gathering was formed around a Covenant of Discipleship, and the class members were accountable for their development as disciples based on living into the covenant agreement. (A contemporary version of that covenant was introduced in our earlier chapter on building the infrastructure of discipling relationships.)

As the class leader asked each member about their faithfulness to the covenant components, an opportunity was provided for teaching, encouragement and support. For example, if a member confessed that he/she was having difficulty living into the part of the covenant related to personal Bible study ("study the Scriptures each day according to a plan"), the Class Leader or the Class might talk about what plan the member was trying to follow, how the plan might be adjusted to make it more workable, what obstacles might remain for living into the plan, and what the member would commit to doing for the next week.

In other words, it was pretty much like a group coaching situation.

Those who excelled in their growth as disciples through the Class Meeting were invited to participate in a Band (the next level of development). There were Men's Bands and Women's Bands. The level of accountability and vulnerability increased exponentially in the Band. For example, instead of talking about how to develop a plan for reading the scriptures, the focus would be on specific temptations the Band members were dealing with and how to overcome them and remain faithful.

As I have participants in my workshops role play using these materials, I usually pick someone that doesn't seem to embarrass easily. Then I explain: In a Band meeting the focus was on "fleeing from the wrath to come." Now this is not a popular message in our day, but in Wesley's time it proved very effective. So the Band leader might say to a participant: "Tom, we exist to help each other flee from the wrath to come through God's Grace. The Evil One is doing everything in his power to draw us away from our commitment. We are constantly being tempted to live in a way that is inconsistent with the life we have been called to live. Sometimes it is to seek forbidden pleasures or to think more highly of ourselves than others, or to judge others, or to engage in the use of substances that are immoral. Would you stand and share with the group all the ways you have been tempted over the past week, so that we can encourage you to stand firm?"

Of course, the response is something like, "You don't really have time for my list!" And we all have a good laugh. But for those in the Bands it was no laughing matter. This sin stuff was serious.

The final level of discipleship in the Wesleyan model was the invitation to participate in a Select Society. Here the 'best of the best' were invited to engage in personal relationships or very small groups for their development as leaders in the Methodist Movement. They were equipped to become

Class Meeting Leaders, Band Leaders, Society Leaders, and Preachers in the Methodist movement. In the interest of complete transparency, there were two types of Select Societies, the one just described and the one no disciple wanted to be invited to. The second of these was focused on remedial training. It was for those disciples who had failed to live into a lifestyle reflecting that of the movement. It was for 'backsliders.'

Wesley's model is still the most successful approach to discipleship in our time. So, let's explore how everything we have talked about is reflected in that model.

Visualizing the Flow

Let's "begin with the end in mind," to again use the language of Stephen Covey. Wesley had clarity about what a Methodist disciple was supposed to be and do. It was summed up in two clearly articulated dimensions:

- Holiness of heart and life.
- Works of mercy.

In the dimension of **holiness of heart and life**, there were clearly articulated behaviors:

- The public worship of God.
- Searching the Scriptures.
- The Lord's Supper (Holy Communion).
- Family and private prayer.
- Christian 'conferencing' (accountable discipleship).
- Fasting or abstinence.

In the dimension of **works of mercy**, the following behaviors were clearly articulated:

- Feeding the hungry.
- Welcoming the stranger.
- Clothing the naked.
- Caring for the sick.
- Visiting the imprisoned.
- Sheltering the homeless.

It is easy to see the way that these behaviors align with the dimensions of spiritual growth that we identified all the way back in chapter one, when we discussed clarity of vision:

A Life of Worship:

✓ The public worship of God.
✓ The Lord's Supper.

A Life of Hospitality:

✓ Christian conferencing.
✓ Welcoming the stranger.

A Life Opening to Jesus:

✓ Searching the Scriptures.
✓ Family and private prayer.
✓ Christian conferencing.

A Life Obeying Jesus:

✓ Christian conferencing.
✓ Searching the Scriptures.

A Life of Service:

✓ Caring for the sick.
✓ Visiting the imprisoned.

A Life of Generosity:

✓ Feeding the hungry.
✓ Clothing the naked.
✓ Sheltering the homeless.

It was a people called Methodists who were living into a life of holiness and mercy (*growing and maturing in the faith*) that engaged a world that was **searching** for meaning in life. Through the lives they lived and the acts of service they offered, people beyond the walls of the church began to discover the love of Jesus Christ. These people were expressions of God's grace to a broken and hurting world. And while there were some notable exceptions, the primary Methodist witness was not actually the preacher at the mines, in the marketplace, or at the cemetery. The primary witness was the everyday Methodist disciple who lived life in accordance with a public commitment. They went to church and prayed and studied Scripture and served and were generous to those in need.

And people responded to these everyday disciples. They wanted to know more about this Jesus who could take ruffians like these and help them discover a 'holiness of heart and life." Some of the people the disciples engaged even asked how to get that for themselves.

They were invited to being **exploring** the faith by coming to a Society meeting. In that setting they witnessed lives that had been changed by the power of God: they heard from people who talked about how God had provided for their greatest needs; they listened to how the Scriptures could be applied to their lives; they prayed for the needs of the communities around them; they experienced the touch of the Holy One. Someone who was further along in the journey than they were had a conversation with them, answered their questions, and walked with them as they decided if the disciple's life was the right thing for them. And some of them decided that this was what they wanted for their own lives. So, they asked what they had to do to be a disciple of Jesus like this.

And they got two answers.

First, if they wanted to be a disciple of Jesus, they could get involved in their local parish. They could go to church. They could become active participants in mission and ministry. After all, Wesley never intended to set up another denomination. In a strong sense, the Methodist movement was a parachurch movement designed to meet a need not being met by the traditional church.

Second, if people were interested in **beginning** a relationship with Jesus through the Methodists, the next step was to become part of a Class Meeting. While this was not a **class** in the modern sense of someone presenting information (lecturer / facilitator) to participants sitting in a circle making copious notes in their workbooks or Bibles, it was a class in the sense of a great deal of instruction taking place, with the practice of key principles being engaged, and accountability for personal application being standard fare. This is where the foundations of the faith were built and theology discussed and spiritual practices formed. The role of the class leader in this setting included coaching and mentoring those who were assigned to his or her care. They even collected an offering, and made time for one-on-one personalized conversations.

For those in the class meetings who were **growing** as disciples, demonstrating lifestyle and behavioral changes reflecting the vision for a people called Methodists, they were invited to be part of a Band or a **small group** where they continued to learn how to live more fully into the fullness of a relationship with Jesus and faithful witness to the world. In the Bands, the participants dug deep, learning how to live as maturing disciples of Jesus. The 'best of the best' in the Bands were invited to participate in Select Societies where the **maturing** disciples were equipped through even smaller groups and one-on-one relationships to become leaders in the Methodist movement—preachers, teachers, class meeting leaders, and band leaders.

Wesley was brilliant! The flow of a discipling process he birthed is the hallmark of the most successful discipleship processes in a variety of traditions today. The non-denominational churches are doing this particularly well. So, for those of us who have yet to establish an accessible, structured framework our own discipleship process, what would such a process look like? Let's begin with the end in mind one more time.

Clarity of Purpose and Goals

Bringing together the examples of the early church, the wisdom of centuries, and best practices gleaned from modern congregations, we have defined a clear set of expectations for the characteristics that define the lifestyle of a maturing disciple.

Maturing disciples will:

- **Live lives honoring God in the ways they work, play, and engage others.**
- **Intentionally build relationships in order to be Christ to someone.**
- **Take responsibility for their own spiritual growth.**
- **Disciple someone else, helping them move toward maturity.**
- **Use their gifts and talents to serve others.**
- **Live within margins in order to bless others.**

Let's summarize all that we have learned from previous chapters about the dimensions of discipleship and the healthy progress from phase to phase.

To engage people in the **searching** phase, disciples from the beginning, growing, and maturing phases build relationships with the ultimate purpose of being Christ in the lives of others whom they encounter. That may include simply being a good friend, a helpful neighbor, a companion in the workplace or serving a need. And some of those people, having seen Christ's love shine through these disciples, may respond by seeking a relationship with God like the one to which their lives bear witness.

For those who are **exploring** the faith—perhaps because of one of the disciples described in the previous paragraph—it is helpful for someone to join them on the journey. They probably know little about the Christian faith, or if they do have some prior connection to Christianity, it may have been a negative experience. Having someone to talk with, ask questions of, and explore possibilities with is the need at this point. Some churches have sponsors or mentors or coaches that fill this role.

For those making a clear commitment to be a disciple, **beginning** the journey creates a profound need to know what is expected of them and to be given instruction in the basics of the faith and introductory spiritual practices. A class setting is probably the least intimidating way to accomplish this. For smaller churches, providing mentors who could walk alongside the new believer is a viable option. This is also the point at which expectations are clearly articulated (e.g. membership covenant, baptism, etc.).

For those **growing** a deeper relationship with Christ, the greatest need is to understand how to live more fully into the life God has offered. This is the time when a variety of educational opportunities are provided to help growing disciples apply the teachings of Jesus to real life. This application of wisdom and habits is greatly enhanced with access to the appropriate type of supportive relationships (e.g. small groups, mentors, discipleship coaches). The typical disciple will spend a significant amount of time in this phase of development relative to the time in the exploring and beginning phases.

Those **maturing** in the faith will always need continuing support in the form of a one-on-one relationship with a mentor, discipleship coach, or spiritual director. While maturing disciples have already formed the basic practices, habits, and lifestyles that reflect their level of faith, there is an ongoing need to pay attention to God at work in their lives and to be faithful (through accountability) to the disciplines necessary to continue deepening their relationship with the Creator. These persons have the maturity to move into leadership roles within their congregations with the proper training and apprenticing.

The graphic on the following page represents a tool that has been built to help people new to your congregation locate themselves on this continuum of movement toward maturity and consider ways that they can continue to grow. It is a helpful resource to start a conversation and help people get connected in formative ways.

CHURCH XYZ

As I follow Jesus,
What's the Next Step for Me?

3 Keys to Growing Spiritually

1. Stay Connected to God

- have a daily time with God
- develop foundational spiritual practices

2. Stay Connected to Others

- invest in Christian friendships
- regularly attend corporate worship
- connect in an accountable relationship
  (mentor, coach, small group)

3. Serve Others

- find a way to serve in the church
- explore ways to serve in the community

Template Provided By:

emc³
LEADERSHIP
COACHING

Phil Maynard, Director
phil@emc3coaching.com

Make maturing disciples of Jesus Christ
for the transformation of the world
(UMC Mission Statement, adapted)

How to Take the Next Step!

1. Review the Spiritual Journey Guide inside.

2. Find out where you are!

3. Identify the one or two steps that will help you grow to the next level.

4. Connect with someone (faith guide, mentor, coach, pastor) and get help.

5. Keep Growing! Make it a priority to grow closer to God and become more like Jesus.

WHERE ARE YOU?

	Guest/Visitor	Regular Worship Attender	Beginning Believer	Growing Disciple	Maturing Disciple / Servant Leader
Is this You?	You have come to check out the church you are attending for the first time or sporadically. You may or may not have accepted Christ as your Savior.	You attend worship regularly or fairly often. You do not participate in the church beyond worship attendance. You may or may not have made a commitment to Christ	You have recently committed or recommitted your life to Christ. You are a new Disciple and want to know more about how to live in this relationship.	You have been a Disciple for a while. You know the basics of the faith, have a daily time with God, engage in some form of accountable discipleship and serve others beyond the church.	You serve sacrificially. You are an influencer and leader in the faith community. You share your faith with those outside the church and disciple someone beginning the journey. You provide leadership in some ministry of the church
How to Grow to the Next Level	Come back. Begin to worship regularly and participate in other ministries of the church.	Commit your life to Christ, engage in conversation with a maturing disciple, form friendships with others in the church, and find a way to serve in a ministry of the church.	Learn about foundational spiritual practices, have a daily devotional time, explore Christian beliefs, connect with other disciples, give proportionately, and find a way to serve in the church.	Commit more of life to following God. Make your spiritual life a priority. Learn about spiritual practices, build relationships beyond the church to share Christ, tithe, and serve beyond the church.	Serve sacrificially in ministry. Continue to grow through spiritual practices, relationships with others, and service. Become a mentor or coach for newer disciples. Lead a ministry.
Things You Can Do to Grow *(select options that meet your needs)*	☐ Learn about the church ☐ Meet people ☐ Ask questions about God ☐ Explore how this church engages the community	☐ Connect with a faith guide ☐ Make a new friend at worship ☐ "Test-drive" a way of serving in the church ☐ Make a commitment to Jesus	☐ Participate in a Foundations Class ☐ Participate in a Beginnings Class ☐ Participate in a Walk to Emmaus ☐ Be baptized ☐ Begin a daily time with God ☐ Serve in a ministry ☐ Begin regular giving	☐ Join a small discipleship group ☐ Attend a Companions in Christ Class ☐ Attend a SHAPE Class ☐ Attend a Financial Peace University Class ☐ Engage in daily spiritual practices ☐ Attend a Disciple Bible Study Class ☐ Tithe ☐ Explore a variety of ways to serve in ministry ☐ Get a Discipleship Coach	☐ Continue to "feed yourself" through spiritual practices ☐ Become a spiritual mentor ☐ Become a Discipleship Coach ☐ Build relationships with non-believers to be Christ in their lives ☐ Provide leadership in an area of ministry ☐ Engage in personal missions ☐ Give generously (beyond a tithe)

Note that the specific activities listed above are just an example from a local congregation. Your congregation may have other ways of supporting disciples in the movement toward maturity. This is simply a template. There is no pre-set expectation or limitation on what your congregation might offer.

I am often asked about the types of activities, relational support, and educational support that might be helpful in the various phases of development. The following graphic takes the six dimensions of discipleship and identifies ways that a congregation might provide support for growing disciples who find themselves in each of the phases of development. Again, this is just a list of possibilities. It is not expected that every church will offer all of these activities and resources. They are provided to 'prime the pump' with your discipleship team as you build a process that will work in your context.

Supporting the Discipling Process

	Exploring	Beginning	Growing	Maturing
A Life of Worship	Witness by worshiping community to the power of faith to transform lives and the community Provide opportunities to engage the local community through service and sharing the Gospel message	Relevant, engaging worship done with excellence Opportunities to make a commitment as a disciple of Jesus Clear next steps in becoming a growing disciple of Jesus Invitations to respond to God in the context of worship experience	Provide passionate corporate worship Give clear next steps for maturing disciples Testimonies in worship Introduction to spiritual disciplines as part of liturgy	Engaged in corporate worship Worship leadership Service in worship to help others engage passionately Model faith-sharing as personal testimonies
A Life of Hospitality	Building of relational connections through hospitality ministries including a hospitality center and hosts/hostesses Personal connection with a mentor/sponsor	Provide Connect/ Life groups to build relationships within church and begin discipleship conversation Encourage invitational hospitality and support with resources Provide entry level activities to encourage invitational hospitality	Training in faith sharing and relational evangelism Provide resources to support invitational hospitality Practice faith-sharing in small groups Celebrate faithfulness in relational/ incarnational hospitality	Encourage building of relationships outside of church Provide training in 'thin places' for personal witnessing Leadership in Connect/ Life Groups
A Life Opening to Jesus	Personal relationship (e.g. sponsor, mentor, faith guide etc.) Conversation with mentor/sponsor around what life as a disciple might/could look like The Lord's Prayer in worship Grace before meals	Foundations Class introducing spiritual practices Alpha/Beginnings Class introducing basic Christian theological understanding Walk to Emmaus – an introduction to theology and practices	Provide in-depth training for: * incarnational hospitality *biblical financial mgmt. *discerning giftedness for service *spiritual disciplines *scriptural reflection/ application Provide a small group ministry supporting the growth of disciples	Practice/explore a wide variety of spiritual disciplines Offer spiritual formation opportunities (classes, retreats) Encourage a relationship with a Discipleship Coach or Spiritual Director Leadership in classes or small groups

A Life Obeying Jesus	Witness by worshipers about the new life discovered in Jesus Conversation with disciple about understanding Grace and God's offer of a relationship through Jesus	Encourage/support a daily devotional time Teach reflection on scripture as life guide Provide opportunities for persons to make a commitment to Jesus in worship, small groups, and individual relationships	Encourage the practice of biblical reflection and life application Model the practice of biblical reflection as a spiritual practice in worship	Train disciples to serve as Discipleship Coaches, mentors, or apprenticers Set clear expectations for discipling others
A Life of Service	Witness by the church about caring for others in the community Participation in community service through church ministries	Offer a variety of opportunities to serve within the church Provide entry ramps for service in the community	Provide a variety of serving opportunities outside the church for disciples to 'try on for size' Offer a resource for discern 'wiring' for service	Support the practice of personal ministries Provide short-term mission experiences Equip leaders for ministries and mission experiences
A Life of Generosity	Witness in church about giving to meet needs in the community Testimonies in worship about lives that have been changed by either giving or receiving	Encourage a pattern of regular giving Develop an awareness of needs and opportunities to make a difference through preaching and teaching	Encourage proportional giving with a movement toward a tithe through preaching/ teaching Provide a biblical financial management class Celebrate/practice acts of kindness and generosity	Encourage tithing as a spiritual practice Equip as trainers for biblical financial management Equip as financial counselors

Questions for Reflection

1. Which model for discipleship would be the best fit for your congregation?

2. Do you already have elements of some of the models discussed in this chapter at work already in your congregation?

3. Can the members of your congregation easily identify the options that are available to them for discipling partnerships? Is there a clear, navigable path for those who want to focus on growth?

4. What systems of accountability are in place within your congregation? For leadership, to keep them focused on growing disciples? For the congregation, to remind them that they are called to grow as disciples?

5. What resources do you have available to 'prime the pump' for those who are interested in growing as disciples? Materials? Reading lists? Web resources? Classes or seminars? Ways to connect directly to explore discipling partnerships?

CONCLUSION

Thank you for joining me on this journey to strengthen the process of intentional discipleship in local congregations. I sincerely believe that at this point in the history of Christ's church—when cultural and technological change is confronting communities of faith as we have known them—there is no greater need than this return to a basic understanding of what it means to become a disciple of Jesus. Technology offers us new tools to connect, and the shifting culture offers us new opportunities to be relevant, but our basic principles and priorities have not changed. There is still no higher calling than helping people discover the fullness of life offered in Jesus Christ.

Now more than ever, we cannot sit back and assume that this process will just happen. Technology offers new tools, but it also offers distractions at an unprecedented pace. The shifting culture offers new opportunities to welcome the marginalized and engage the creative, but it also is increasingly confident that it doesn't need us (or God) at all.

So our work continues, and it requires a thoughtful and organized approach. It is not easy work. It will take time. But it will be worth the effort, and by doing the required work, we will deepen our own relationships with Christ and with our fellow disciples, and we will be renewed in our purpose and passion in connecting to the world around us—a world that desperately needs the message of hope that is the Good News.

Don't try to build all of this at once, and don't feel that you are trapped in any one particular template. We have provided core principles and many specific examples from actual faith communities. Although these principles of discipleship hold true for congregations of different sizes and resources, historical and cultural settings, and theological shadings, there are many strategies for embracing them and successfully living them out. Take the time to understand what will work with your unique congregation. Don't be afraid to abandon what isn't working and try a different approach. But above all, have a clearly defined approach that is owned by your leadership, understood by your congregation, and established as a part of the identity of your community of believers.

We encourage you to continue to utilize the resources of Excellence in Ministry Coaching and other parachurch organizations that provide resources and a forum for discussion. We welcome your feedback as to what's working for you and where the challenges lie, and together we will continue to bear much good fruit for God's kingdom.

Blessings on your own personal journey of discipleship,

Dr. Phil Maynard

NOTES

CHAPTER 1— CLARITY

1. George Barna and Timothy Jones, *The Saints Among Us,* 1999, Moorehouse Publishing, as quoted by Stephen Lim in blog "Why Churches Don't Disciple and How Yours Can," http://enrichmentjournal.ag.org/200801/200801_048_WhyChDon't.cfm.
2. George Barna, *Growing True Disciples: New Strategies for Producing Genuine Followers of Christ,* Waterbrook Press, 2001, p. 82.
3. George Barna and Timothy Jones, *The Saints Among Us,* George Barna and Timothy Jones, 1999, Moorehouse Publishing, as quoted by Stephen Lim in blog "Why Churches Don't Disciple and How Yours Can." http://enrichmentjournal.ag.org/200801/200801_048_WhyChDon't.cfm.
4. George Barna, *Growing True Disciples: New Strategies for Producing Genuine Followers of Christ,* Waterbrook Press, 2001, pp27-28.
5. Dallas Willard, *The Great Omission,* HarperSanFrancisco, 2006, pp. 5-6.
6. Dallas Willard, *The Divine Conspiracy: Rediscovering Our Hidden Life in God*, Harper, 1998, pp26-27.
7. dictionaryofchristianese.com.
8. Shift quote is found on pages 65-66, *Shift: Helping Congregations Back Into the Game of Effective Ministry, 2013, Phil Maynard*
9. Albert L. Winseman, *Growing An Engaged Church,* Gallup Press, 2007, pp. 84-85.
10. Medina UMC, Medina OH, www.medinaumc.com , shared by Pastor David Tennant.
11. Evergreen Church, Leesburg, VA, www.evergreenchurch.net, shared by Pastor Chip Giessler.

CHAPTER 2 – MOVEMENT

1. Jim Putman in his book, *Real Life Discipleshp: Building Churches That Make Disciples,* NavPress, 2010.
2. Greg L. Hawkins and Cally Parkinson, *Move: What 1,000 Churches Reveal about Spiritual Growth*, Zondervan, 2011.

CHAPTER 3 – MINISTRY AS CONTACT SPORT

1. http://saddleback.com/connect [Baseball diamond illustration--this is an archived web page—no longer in active publication.]
2. http://saddleback.com/connect/ministry/class [this is an archived web page—no longer in active publication.]
3. First UMC Jacksonville, class schedule printout, circa 2013.
4. https://www.google.com/?gws_rd=ssl#q=laissez+faire+definition.

5. Greg Ogden, *Transforming Discipleship*, IVP Books, 2003, p. 140.

6. Greg Ogden, *Transforming Discipleship*, IVP Books, 2003, pp. 141-142.

7. Greg Ogden, *Transforming Discipleship*, IVP Books, 2003, pp 145-149.

8. Kevin Watson, *The Class Meeting*, location 421 (Kindle version).

9. Reggie McNeal, *Missional Renaissance*, Jossey-Bass, 2009, pp. 95-99.

10. Tom Bandy, *Christian Mentoring*, Bandy Books, 2011, pp. 57-126.

11. Chad Hall, Bill Copper, and Kathryn McElveen, *Faith Coaching*, Coach Approach Ministries, 2009, p. 35.

12. Margaret Guenther, *Holy Listening: The Art of Spiritual Direction*, Cowley Publications, 1992, pp. 141-142.

13. Greg Hawkins and Cally Parkinson, *Reveal: Where Are You?*, Willow Creek Association, 2007, p. 53.

14. Greg Hawkins and Cally Parkinson, *Reveal: Where Are You?*, WillowCreek Association, 2007, p. 53.

15. Albert L. Winseman, *Growing An Engaged Church*, Gallup Press, 2007, pp.106-107.

16. Reggie McNeal, *Missional Renaissance: Changing the Scorecard for the Church,* Jossey-Bass, 2009, p. 98.

CHAPTER 4 – EQUIPPING FOR TRANSFORMATION

1. Phil Maynard, *Connect*, www.emc3coaching.com.

2. Bob Farr, Kay Kotan, and Doug Anderson, G*et Their Name: Grow Your Church by Building New Relationships,* Abingdon Press, 2013, pp. 5-25.

3. Louie Giglio, *Wired for a Life of Worship*, Multnomah Publishers, 2006, pp. 138-139.

4. Nicky Gumbel. The Alpha Initiative, *Telling Others,* by Nicky Gumbel, David C. Cook Publishing, 1994.

5. Andy Langford and Mark Ralls, *Beginnings: An Introduction to Christian Faith,* Abingdon Press, 2003.

6. Matt Redmon, *Unquenchable Worshipper,* Regal Books, 2001.

7. Jack Hayford, *Worship His Majesty,* Regal Books, 2000.

8. Christine Pohl, *Making Room: Recovering Hospitality as a Christian Tradition,* Eerdmans Publishing Co., 1999.

9. Bob Farr, Kay Kotan, and Doug Anderson, *Get Their Name: Growing Your Church by Building New Relationships,* Abingdon Press, 2013.

10. Ken Sande and Kevin Johnson, *Resolving Everyday Conflict,* Baker Books, 2015.

11. Jim Van Yperen, *Living in Authentic Community,* Metanoia Ministries, www.restoringthechurch.org.

12. Phil Maynard, *Connect: Equipping Congregations to Be Christ and Share Christ in   the World,* www.emc3coaching.com. [Available Fall 2015.]

13. Rueben Job, Marjorie J Thompson, and E Glenn Hinson, *Companions in Christ,* Upper Room Bookstore, 2006, bookstore.upperroom.org.

14. Richard Foster, *Prayer: Finding the Heart's True Home,* Zondervan Press, 2002

15. Ken Gire, *The Reflective Life,* Chariot Victor Publishing, 1998

16. *Discipleship Coaching Training.* Church Leadership Training Institute, www.churchleadershiptraining.com.

17. Eric Rees, SHAPE, Zondervan, 2006

18. *PLACE: Finding Your Place in Life and Ministry,* www.placeministries.wazala.com.

19. Adam Hamilton, *Enough: Discovering Joy Through Simplicity and Generosity,* Abingdon Press, 2009.

20. Dave Ramsey, *Financial Peace University,* www.daveramsey.com.

CHAPTER 5 – PUTTING THE PIECES TOGETHER

1. Adapted from *Transforming Discipleship* by Greg Ogden, IVP Books, 2003, p.82

2. Greg Ogden, *Transforming Discipleship,* IVP Books, 2003, p. 105.

3. Marcia Ford, *Traditions of the Ancients: Vintage Faith Practices for the 21st Century,* B&H Publishing Group, 2006, p. 61.

4. *The Journal of John Wesley,* Christian Classics Ethereal Library, www.ccel.org.